THE SEVEN DEADLY SINS
AND THE
SEVEN HEAVENLY VIRTUES

The Seven Sins and Seven Virtues as seen in
World Religion, Mythology and Art and Literature

BY
JULIAN BOUND

Novels by Julian Bound

Subway of Light
Life's Heart Eternal
The Geisha and The Monk
The Soul Within
Of Futures Past
A Gardener's Tale
By Way of The Sea
Four Hearts
All Roads

Story Collections

Of Eden's Touch
Ten Minute Travels

Non-Fiction

In the Field
The Mindfulness of Wandering
The Seven Deadly Sins and The Seven Heavenly Virtues

Julian Bound

CONTENTS

Julian Bound

INTRODUCTION

The Seven Deadly Sins and the antidotes of The Seven Heavenly Virtues have been depicted throughout history in forms of both Greek and Roman mythology and in art and literature.

Predominantly perceived as being associated within the doctrine of the Christian faith, examples of the seven sin's transgressions can be found in the belief systems of other religions of the world, as can remedies held in the seven virtues.

This book is the result of a four year journey across eight countries observing the parallels between the religions of Asia and South East Asia and that of the Western world.

Witnessing the practice of Buddhism in the countries of Tibet, Bhutan, Nepal, Thailand, Cambodia, Laos and Myanmar, and the array of religions present within India, from Hinduism and Sikhism to the Portuguese influence of Catholicism amid the palm trees and beaches of the western coastlines of India, sins and virtues played a major role in reverence held towards the many Gods, Goddesses and Deities encountered.

In exploring the remote high altitude Buddhist temples of Tibet, the riverside fortress monasteries of Bhutan and the sun drenched golden temples of South East Asia, it could be seen how all branches of Buddhism adhered to the same line of thought, to escape suffering by acts of kindness.

This philosophy was shared by the religions of Nepal and India, where brightly coloured temples adorned with effigies of Gods and Goddesses told of sin's corruption and of divine acts of generosity given to another soul, with Sikhism also expressing benevolence and compassion within the sacred grounds of the Golden Temple in the heart of the Punjab.

The theology of each religion expressed similar messages echoing precepts found in faiths of the western civilisation.

The purpose of this book is not only to examine said similarities between religions of the world or as a study of the sins and virtues, but for the reader to identify which sin they are prone to and of what virtue best displays their greatest qualities; the result of which is an exploration of the self within the concept of the facets of the seven sins and seven virtues, and so aiding progression along each soul's unique individual path.

Julian Bound

THE FIRST DEADLY SIN

LUST

Noun: lust / ˈlʌst/
An overpowering sexual desire.
'her lust for him was soon returned.'
Synonyms: sexual appetite, sexual longing,
Lustfulness, ardour, desire, passion.

'The lust for comfort, that stealthy thing that enters the house a guest, and then becomes a host, and then a master.'

Khalil Gibran

AN INTRODUCTION TO LUST

From Cupid's mischievous antics of bestowing the unexpected with passion tipped arrows, to Rati, the Hindu Goddess of sensual pleasures whose prowess in the art of sexual technique contributed to the ancient script of the Karma Sutra, the deadly sin of lust has been embedded in the human psyche throughout history.

Defined by the Christian Church as an emotion of intense sensual desire and an unbridled want for material possessions, lust is regarded in other world religions as the most destructive of sins.

Buddhist teachings speak of the want for sensual pleasure as being one of the 'Three Poisons' and so becoming an unwholesome root of being.

Hinduism confirms Buddhism's principles in that lust is observed as the greatest threat to the whole of humanity.

Represented in both Greek and Roman mythology as a main driving force of Gods, Goddesses and Deities, the frequency of lust in the performance and the desire for attractive mortals saw those residing on Mount Olympus submitting to the throws of passion administered by lust time and time again.

As in mythology and legend the arts found lust to be of great influence. Artists of the Baroque and Renaissance periods took the theme of sensual desire to heart in their portrayal of the sin from folk law and Biblical parables.

This fascination with lustfulness of the soul continued into the early twentieth century with the emergence of the surrealist movement, where it would be allegorised by prominent artists such as Dali, Ernst, Magritte and Tanguy.

Classic literature would also utilise lust as a theme as was shown in the works of Venetian writer Giacomo Casanova, and Pierre Choderlos de Laclos in his eighteenth century homage to the disparaging forces of lust 'Les Liaisons Dangereuses'.

In theology, lust is seen as an eternal battle within the heart of humankind, yet it is its disassociation with love which defines the sin. For if lust is in turn reciprocated under the mantle of love between two souls, then the deadly sin can, for a time at least, be dissolved from the spirit.

LUST IN RELIGION

CHRISTIANITY

'For all that is in the world - the desires of the flesh and the desires of the eyes and pride in possessions - is not from the Father but is from the world.'
John 2: 16

Even though the two are inevitably linked, the Christian Church divides the powerful emotions of lust and passion.

With passion reserved for the purposes of Heavenly realms and the core of God's will, lust is regarded as a sensual desire expressed in an overly inappropriate manner.

In the general consensus of identifying lust with that of sexual pleasures another facet of the sin is recognised within the church. As well as considering lust in its form of sexual context, a desire for material trappings and wealth also portray the sin in an individual's insatiable lust of wants and needs. These wants are often perceived as being able to bring happiness into their life, which only leads to amplifying the inherent elements found within lust.

The identification of lust reaches further in the eyes of the Catholic Church, where it is deemed as one of the most abhorrent of sins.

Believed to devalue the essence of love between two people, lust is ultimately condemned when employed in a sexual situation outside the marital grounds of wedlock.

Examples of the intense emotional suffering caused by being in lust's grasp are expressed in by the 4th century theologian, Saint Augustine of Hippo.

Born in Algeria in 354BC and regarded as the patron of doves, pens and that of the pierced heart, St. Augustine is revered for his writings on the theology of sexuality within the human condition.

Consisting of thirteen volumes, Augustine's autobiographical 'The Confessions' is an account of his promiscuity during his formative years.

Written in his early forties and regarded as the most detailed account of life in the 4th century, The Confessions can be viewed as Augustine's purging of lust before continuing his life in surrender to God.

Augustine's subsequent book 'The City of God' would give an additional insight into lust, in that the deadly sin causes a division of faith. Portraying the battle of good versus evil both in the internal ways of the soul and externally in the physical world in the form of warring, Augustine goes further in suggesting that lust was an important factor in the instigation of Adam and Eves expulsion from the Garden of Eden.

These thoughts would soon be adopted and absorbed by the Catholic Church, and so bringing about the complete repulsion of the sin of lust and its effects upon its followers.

BUDDHISM

'He who subdues himself shall be free; he shall cease to be a slave of passions. The righteous man casts off evil, and by rooting out lust, bitterness, and illusion do we reach Nirvana.'
Gautama Buddha

Lust within Buddhism is regarded as an aspect of attachment, in the sense that a desire for sensual pleasure leads to suffering of the mind when not received.

This can be seen in the Buddhist doctrine of the 'Four Noble Truths' which tells of Buddha's guidelines of realising there is suffering in life, the causes of suffering, and escape of suffering by adhering to the correct actions observed in the 'Eight Fold Path'.

The Four Noble Truths

Dukkha – The truth of suffering.
Samudata –The truth of the cause of suffering.
Nirodha –The truth of the end of suffering.
Magga – The truth of the path that frees us from suffering.

It is Samudata that identifies the shortcomings of lust as one of the root causes of suffering experienced by the soul. This is recognised in the arising of Tanha within the Buddha's second Noble Truth.

Derived from the Sanskrit word Tarsa, the concepts of Tanha are the desire or thirst for wealth, material goods, and as in the case of lust, a craving for physical pleasure.

The act of Tanha is furthered by being broken down into the three characteristics: Kama-tanha – a craving for sensual pleasures, Bhava-tanha – a want of existing, and Vibhava-tanha – the craving for non-existence of mind.

It is within the clinging to these wants and desires found in lust which leads to suffering by retaining attachment to both physical and emotional properties, and so hindering a soul's escape from the endless cycle of life, death and rebirth.

In the Mahayana Buddhist tradition of Tibetan Buddhism, lust can be defined as Chanda - a holding of the excitement or desire to act, and can also be associated to one of the Three Poisons found in the hub of the Wheel of Life in Buddhist teaching.

Represented by a pig, Moha - ignorance, provides momentum for the Wheel of Life's impetus of reincarnation.

With each poison leading to the creation of karma in an individual's lifetime and all subsequent lifetimes thereafter, Moha is accompanied by a cockerel, Lobha - greed, and the snake, Dvesha – hatred.

These three creatures represent the root of all evil as found in humanity and from where all sins arise. Also known in Buddhism as the 'Roots of Unhappiness', it is Moha's representation of ignorance of the soul that refers not only to the attachment of physical objects and tendencies towards avarice, but also to the emotions of lust and the overreaching need for sensual pleasure.

HINDUISM

'It is lust alone, which is born of contact with the mode of passion, and later transformed into anger. Know this as the sinful, all-devouring enemy in the world.'
The Bhagavad Gita

Regarded as a great threat not only to Hindu devotees but to the whole of humanity, lust in Hinduism is known as being one of the doorways to Naraka, the Hindu equivalent to Hell, where Yama, the God of Death watches over all sinners consigned to his home and are tormented for the vices committed during their lifetime.

Expressing the embodiment of lust Hindu scripture denotes the Goddess Rati to such duties.

Mounted on a colourful parrot and wielding a sword, Rati's attribute of lust is accompanied by the traits of carnal passions and the overindulgence of sexual pleasures.

Represented in the art history of the Hindu belief system, Rati is shown as holding a unique beauty of which enhances her sensuality, and so adds to her allure towards those submitting to lust's pull on the senses.

Companion, consort and as is suggested a concubine to Kamadeva, the Hindu God of love and sexual attraction, his name deriving from the Sanskrit - 'Kama' meaning longing of sexual desire, and 'Deva' – the Divine, Rati is believed to be the instigator of arousal leading to sexual expression within humankind.

With the Sanskrit word Kama equating to sexual desire, the ancient Hindu text of the Kama Sutra holds a connection with the Goddess of Lust amongst its 1,250 verses, with many of the titles of the sexual positions contained within derived from Rati's name due to her association with sexual techniques and taste for sensuous desire.

LUST IN MYTHOLOGY

GREEK

With stories of Greek Gods and Goddesses leaving Mount Olympus to satisfy their sexual desires with any earthbound human that took their fancy, Greek mythology is besieged with acts of lust in both mortal and immortal realms.

Himeros the God of Sexual desire, Pothos, God of Sexual yearning, Peitho, the personification of Seduction, and Pan, consort of Nymphs and famed for his sexual prowess, cloven hoofed feet and constantly erect phallus, are just some of the many examples of how Grecian myths portrayed the undesirable traits of the deadly sin of lust. Yet there is one certain winged God who represents the affliction of lust upon humanity.

Aphrodite the Goddess Love, Pleasure and Procreation, and her union with Ares the Greek God of War, sometimes depicted as the half-brother of Aphrodite, resulted in the birth of Eros, the God of Sexual allure and Desirability.

Taking the form of a winged boy, his infamous bow and arrow at the ready in his hands, Eros was known for his mischievous antics in the regard of inflicting love on the unexpected, but he was also equally known for his disobedience. This rebellious nature led to Eros inflicting lust within others, much to the anger of the Gods.

Having the utmost devotion for his mother, Aphrodite was the only one who could calm her son and rectify his misdeeds, and so was called upon frequently by the disgruntled Gods of Mount Olympus who had encountered Eros' barbed arrow of lust.

ROMAN

As with Greek mythology, the ancient Romans also had several Gods and Goddesses denoting the sin of lust and it's far reaching connotations.

Suadela, the Roman Goddess of Seduction from highly tuned persuasive methods, proved her abilities in the fields of love and romance, whereas Voluptas was known for her Goddess like powers of sensual pleasure, hence her name, Voluptas deriving from the Latin, pleasure, delight and that of entertainment.

Voluptas would be invariably linked to Venus, the Goddess of Desire within sex and love in Roman mythology.

As Aphrodite's Roman complement, Venus was in turn the mother of Eros' counterpart Cupid. As like Eros, Cupid showed the same devotion to his mother and it is said that Venus was also the only one who could still her son's mischievous acts of inflicting lust on the unexpected.

Voluptas' connection with Venus would come about not only from being found on occasion accompanying the Three Graces of Joy, Celebration and Kindness, but in being a granddaughter to the Goddess of Love.

Born of the union between Cupid and Psyche, who was allowed immortality as a reward for her sexual love and the virginity she surrendered to Cupid's lust, Voluptas' place within the Roman hierarchy of lust was so confirmed.

LUST IN ART AND LITERATURE

THE TEMPTATION OF ST. ANTHONY
SALVADOR DALI

Salvador Dali's 1946 oil painting 'The Temptation of St. Anthony' can be appreciated as an allegory to the enticements and desires of Lust.

The early twentieth century Spanish surrealist painter executed his high standard of technical ability to portray sexual longing as an integral characteristic within humanity. With the use of symbolism and subtle undertones of sexual frustration, Dali conveys St. Anthony's journey into the Arabian Desert after his renouncing of all worldly pleasures.

Drawing on his faith in his pursuit for God, the third century Christian monk was given to hallucinations in his solitary quest. These visions would be presented to him by dark forces which abhorred Anthony's devout worship of God, and were portrayed as the joys and pleasures of which St. Anthony missed most.

Dali presents St. Anthony as a naked dishevelled figure kneeling in the left corner of a barren desert landscape. His hand aloft, he directs a small basic wooden crucifix towards his hallucinogenic vision of a caravan of three impossibly long legged elephants led by a teeth clenched rearing white horse of similar dimensions.

In signifying voluptuousness and power, the horse is at the forefront of the parade, with each following elephant carrying cyphers on their saddled backs denoting facets of lust.

Balanced precariously on the back of the first elephant, a naked woman in erotic stance stands within a gold gilded cup of lust, her hair flowing carelessly in the wind symbolising abandonment of chastity. Mounted on the back of the second elephant a phallic shaped obelisk raises up to blue skies, whilst the beast behind carries buildings in the style of the sixteenth century Italian architect Andrea Palladio, whose constructions were influenced by the ostentatious erections of ancient Roman and Grecian architecture.

On the far horizon a fourth elephant carries another phallic symbol in the representation of a tall thin stone walled tower, above which tempestuous cloud formations hold glimpses of El Escorial, the monastery of San Lorenzo, on the outskirts of Madrid. It is in his perception of the rooftops of El Escorial that St. Anthony is given hope in overcoming temptation whilst bombarded with visions of lust.

The Garden of Earthly Delights
Hieronymus Bosch

Hieronymus Bosch's sixteenth century oak panelled triptych 'The Garden of Earthly Delights' portrays lust more than any other of the seven deadly sins. With depictions of the sin scattered throughout the composition, this is regarded as being influenced by the artists own revulsion towards lust and the holding of chastity in his life.

The first panel represents God's gift of Eden to Adam and Eve, the middle panel shows the delights of Creation as perceived in Biblical terms, with the final third panel revealing the damnation and torment of a sinful Hellscape.

The centre panel of the triptych is an extension of Eden's garden of lush greenery and pools of calm water under a blue summer sky. Filled with hoards of frolicking nude figures and fanciful animals, strange giant fruits are dispersed throughout the composition.

Although at first sight Bosch's central panel illustrates an idyllic life without the presence of sin and debauchery, yet it can be observed that the scene acts as the artist's warning towards the moral jeopardy of submitting to sin, most notably that of lust.

This can be viewed in the portrayal of nakedness and the carefree antics of all present, displaying subtleties of selfishness in their apparent want for only the pleasures in life. This can be defined by the presence of several oversized fruits amid the painting. Equated to sins of the flesh, these are represented as either containing people within them or in being coveted by others.

It is in the third panel that Bosch's subtlety in illustrating lust is banished and is shown in full display.

From the naked woman sitting beneath the bird headed Prince of Hell, a toad resting on her breast denoting the connotations of lust held within a lifetime spent in vanity, to the gigantic ears towards the top section of the panel, where dissected by a large knife, leads to signify the lure of lust's needs of unrivalled passion in its metaphorical representation of the male genitalia.

Such is the complexity of 'The Garden of Earthly Delights'

examples of lust can be identified in all aspects of the painting, thus providing a dominant theme throughout the piece. The temptation and human desire of lustfulness would be administered three hundred years later in the surrealist movement of the early twentieth century, marking Hieronymus Bosch as not only a forerunner, but perchance attaining the right of being the first surrealist painter in art history.

The Divine Comedy: Inferno
Dante Alighieri

In Dante Alighieri's fourteenth century 'Divine Comedy', lust is encountered in 'Inferno' the first part of the classic three episodic saga.

After leaving Limbo's dominion and guided by the Roman poet Virgil, Dante is taken to the second circle of Hell to meet with those who have lived a lifetime overcome with lust.

Virgil and Dante watch those once consumed by the sin being blown back and forth along the terrace on which they now stand. Explaining the reasoning behind the voracity held within the gales, Virgil tells Dante the winds signify the restlessness harboured within the soul of an individual under the influence of lust, and whose desires were largely lead by the pleasures of the flesh.

It is on their arrival to Hell's second circle of lust that Virgil and Dante observe figures from history being buffeted by the winds of lust. Cleopatra and the Greek hero Achilles are cast across the terrace, as are Helene of Troy and her lover Paris, both of whose wanton lust for one another instigated the Trojan War resulting in the deaths of thousands.

Les Liaisons Dangereuses
Pierre Choderlos de Laclos

First published in 1782 as a set of four volumes, Pierre Choderlos de Laclos' 'Les Liaisons Dangereuses', symbolises the complexity of lust when administered in the territories of adultery and social standing.

Focusing on the tumultuous relationship of former lovers, the Marquise of Merteuil and the Viscount of Valmont, the rivalry between the two within the eyes of the French aristocracy leads them to use lust and sexual indiscretions as means of not only one-upmanship but in order to satisfy a want of the humiliation of another.

With the novel's prose comprising of a series of letters written by the characters to one another, a tale of the immorality and misdeeds of those of a high social circle play with those of the lower classes unfolds, where the corruption and taking away of innocence becomes a manipulative game for the Marquise and Viscount.

As the sin of lust consumes each in their want for the pleasures of demeaning another's soul, the tragedies which ensue are construed as an ethical warning towards others who too fall foul of the shallow delights lustfulness can present.

THE FIRST HEAVENLY VIRTUE

CHASTITY

Noun: chastity / ˈtʃastɪti/
The refraining from extramarital or all sexual intercourse.
'Her chastity was significant.'
Synonyms: virginity, abstinence, self-restraint, celibacy, chasteness,
purity, virtue.

*'A nun of winter's sisterhood kisses not more religiously; the very ice of chastity is
in them.'*

William Shakespeare, As You Like It

An Introduction to Chastity

Regarded as the antidote to the deadly sin of Lust, Chastity is observed in all religions across the world.

From finding place amid the many precepts towards reaching enlightenment in Buddhist teachings to Hinduism's first stage of a Hindu's journey through life, acts of chastity have been documented since the beginning of civilisation.

Often taken to the extremes in western cultures, ranging from either showing a modicum of restraint to a total abandonment of procreation, these extremes are inborn within most traditions of the northern hemisphere.

With chastity viewed as by living a pure life then an individual shall be pure of heart, artists have depicted the virtue over the centuries, their focus given to those of Mount Olympus and the eternal battle between Gods, Goddesses and Nymphs representing acts of love and passion and those Deities who hold chastity to them as a guiding light to their existence and influence on Earth's mere mortals.

Chastity in Religion

Christianity

'But I say to you that everyone who looks at a woman with lustful intent has already committed adultery with her in his heart.'
Matthew 5: 28

Chastity in the views of the Christian Church is centred on the practice and refinement of a sexual purity deemed acceptable in the observation of God.

In stilling the values of fidelity within the sanctum of marriage, any form of sensual misconduct before married life is seen as breaking the qualities of chastity and of what the virtue implies.

It is in the Catholic Church that the theology of chastity is expanded.

With the Sixth Commandment's instruction of not partaking in marital affairs, it is the eternal separation from God that keeps a Catholic from breaking their vow of chastity.

As being viewed as an unnatural act of human sexuality in the eyes of God, contraception is considered a crime towards chastity and as representing an infringement of the Heavenly virtue.

The Catholic abstinence of contraception is not adhered to by those of Anglican faith; although some restrictions are placed upon the Anglican branch of Christianity in that the relative size of a family is taken into consideration.

Unlike the Anglican clerics who are encouraged to marry and procreate, priests of the Catholic order are called upon to abstain fully in any form of sensual contact and pleasures of a sexual nature.

The United Society of Believers in Christ's Second Coming took the virtue of chastity to its far extremes.

Known as the Shakers and founded in the eighteenth century, those who converted to the Shakers were told to refrain from sex outright. This resulted in a totally puritanical society whose only means of continual growth came from new converts or through adoption.

BUDDHISM

'A wise man should avoid lust as if it were a burning pit of live coals. From the contact comes sensation, from sensation thirst, from thirst clinging; by ceasing from that, the soul is delivered from all sinful existence.'
Gautama Buddha

With the differing branches of Buddhism, be it Daoism, Jainism, or the Theravada and Mahayana schools of Buddhist teaching, chastity is observed by those who live a monastic life and have taken refuge in the ways of the Buddha.

In the Tibetan Buddhist tradition of Mahayana Buddhism, leading on from the Four Noble Truths, the precepts of The Eight Fold Path act as a guide in was of reaching enlightenment and escaping the suffering of rebirth within Earthly realms.

The Eight Fold Path

1. Right view: The belief that there is no death and that Buddha took a successful path to find enlightenment and enter the realm of nirvana.
2. Right resolve: The adoption of a life of a religious journey with no ill will to all sentient beings.
3. Right speech: Not telling one person what another says and not telling lies of using profanities in speaking.
4. Right action: No killing or injuring others, not taking what is not given and no sexual acts.
5. Right livelihood: Working only for sustenance with no livelihood that can cause to others, such as warfare and gun running.
6. Right effort: Protecting the mind against unwholesome thoughts that may hinder the act of meditation.
7. Right mindfulness: Always paying attention and being aware of what you are doing, and understanding the impermanence of body, mind and emotions.
8. Right concentration (Samadhi): Cultivating the stages of Dhyana meditation.

It is in The Eight Fold Path's teaching of 'Right action' that the ideology of chastity can be found. This, the Path's fourth guideline, directs a devotee to The Five Precepts and the moral acts found therein.

Followers of Buddha who adhere to The Five Precepts are referred to as Upasaka (masculine) and Upasika (feminine), their titles taken from the ancient Sanskrit word for 'attendant'.

Upasaka or Upasika are regarded as a Buddhist who does not lead a monastic life as a monk or a nun yet still revers the teachings of Buddha, of which The Five Precepts are held for them, with the third precept referring to chastity.

The Five Precepts

1. I will not take the life of a sentient being.
2. I will not take what has not been given to me.
3. I will refrain from sexual misconduct.
4. I will refrain from false speech.
5. I will refrain from becoming intoxicated.

For those who have chosen to surrender to life as being a Buddhist monk or nun, then the terms Bhikkhu (masculine) and Bhikkhuni (feminine) are used to reflect the devotion of a devotee who lives a monastic lifestyle that leads to the adherence of The Eight Precepts.

The Eight Precepts

1. I undertake the precept to refrain from destroying living creatures.
2. I undertake the precept to refrain from taking that which is not given.
3. I undertake the precept to refrain from sexual activity.
4. I undertake the precept to refrain from incorrect speech.
5. I undertake the precept to refrain from intoxicating drinks and drugs.
6. I undertake the precept to refrain from eating at the forbidden time.
7. I undertake the precept to refrain from dancing, singing and music.
8. I undertake the precept to refrain from lying on a luxurious sleeping place.

The total abstinence of sensual pleasure and avoidance of any form of sexual activity is identified in the third precept, bringing a vow of celibacy to the chaste lives of a Buddhist monk or nun.

HINDUISM

'Keep your mind pure, for what a person thinks, he becomes—this is the eternal mystery... When the mind is silent... you can transcend the mind.'
Maitri Upanishad

Chastity in Hinduism is seen as one of the four stages of life and is regarded as being the correct moral characteristic of male and female students before partaking in the sanctity of marriage.

Translated from the Latin, castitas, Brahmacharya is regarded as the definition of chastity, which is observed in a Hindu's devotion towards Shiva, 'The Auspicious One' and one of the foremost divinities of Hinduism alongside Brahma the Creator, and Vishnu the Preserver.

Brahmacharya can be translated as Brahma – the collective knowledge of the self, and Charya – the leading of an honourable way of existence, and is considered as the first stage of the four steps of Ashrama in a sentient being's lifetime. The Ashrama system of age related junctures of time are as follows:

Brahmacharya – the life of a student: Until the age of 24.
Grihastha – household life: 24 to 48 years.
Vanaprastha – retired life: 48-72 years.
Sannyasa – renounced life: 72 years until death.

Denoting the unmarried life of male and female students until the age of twenty-four years, the stage of Brahmacharya is focused on the cultivation of chastity in the forms of practicing celibacy and concentrating on education of the mind that includes that of Hindu theology.

This step of chaste living and being steeped in the values found within Hindu scripture alongside the instruction of the sciences and the philosophies of the world, teaches its student good ethical standing in the art of self-discipline and the avoidance of lust within the soul.

Through the practice and refinement of chastity a student of Brahmacharya is then deemed ready to enter the second stage of Ashrama, that being when a devotee steps into marriage and the duties held within in the raising and educating of their children, providing for their family, and conducting a life within the constructs of virtuous living.

CHASTITY IN MYTHOLOGY

GREEK

The daughter of Zeus, King of the Gods, and Leto, Goddess of Demure and Womanhood, Artemis, the Greek Goddess of Chastity was born on the island of Ortega with her twin brother Apollo the God of Art, Oracles and Plague.

Regarded in ancient Greek mythology as being the personification of Virginity and the patron of Chastity, Artemis was borne of Leto when the Goddess of Demure was in hiding from Zeus' vengeful wife, Hera.

The scenario surrounding the circumstances of Artemis' birth would add to her attributes of Chastity and the Moon, in that of the Hunt.

Protector of women and having the ability to release diseases prone to womanhood, Artemis is often portrayed in mural and sculpture as carrying a bow and accompanying arrows in the wilderness of ancient Greece.

ROMAN

The counterpart of the Greek Goddess Artemis, Diana would take the role of Chastity in the eyes of those of ancient Rome.

Known also for her patronage of hunting, Diana's virtue towards that of chaste living was further progressed in her involvement with Egeria, the Nymph and concubine of Pompilius, the second King of Rome, and an assistant midwife, and Virbius, who armed with a sword, worshiped Diana and was deemed the God of Woodlands and defender therefor of.

This trio of Goddess, God and Nymph, became defenders of sacred woods and forests, often depicted resting at the foothills of mountains.

The Divine Celestial collaboration of Diana, Egeria and Virbius, would also be depicted as offering protection to those who ventured into their sacred domains when hunting, or of the women who entered woodland areas to worship Diana when struck with problems in conceiving or in fear of difficulties in childbirth.

Often depicted with a pack of hunting dogs at her feet, dressed in a short tunic and carrying a cyprus wood bow, Diana's portrayal of a huntress would match the youthful beauty of Venus, and even though such attractiveness attracted the attention of many a lustful God, Diana retained her composure and her vow of chastity.

CHASTITY IN ART AND LITERATURE

BURIAL OF ST. LUCY
CARAVAGGIO

Caravaggio's 1608 painting 'Burial of St. Lucy' portrayed the effects of faith given strength in an individual under the Holy inspiration of Chastity.

The painting depicts the body of St. Lucy, who after giving away her money to the poor, was denounced as a Christian during the Great Persecution of Christians in the Roman Empire.

Refusing to reject her beliefs in Christianity, St. Lucy offered her chastity to Christ and was so condemned by the Roman authorities to be taken to work in a brothel.

As Roman centurions attempted to transport her to the brothel, they found that St. Lucy could not be moved from her spot.

Such was the anger caused by God's intervention that she was pierced in the throat by a knife, and where she fell, the church of Santa Lucia al Sepolcro was built in the city of Syracuse, on the island of Sicily.

Depicting St. Lucy laying on the floor whilst two men begin digging her grave beside her, surrounded by mourners and overlooked by members of the clergy, Caravaggio's use of ochre and burnt sienna tones in his painting brings a subtle sense of romance towards the situation, with the ordained figure positioned in the centre of the piece adding to St. Lucy's act of martyrdom in the wearing of blood red clothing.

COMBAT OF LOVE AND CHASTITY
PIETRO PERUGINO

Painted in 1503 by the Italian Renaissance artist Pietro Perugino, Combat of Love and Chastity (sometimes referred to as The Battle of Love and Chastity) depicts a clash between the mythological representations of Love and Chastity.

With a backdrop of hills and the waters of a calm river, the autumnal scene features the battle in the foreground of the painting.

In the centre of the piece Venus, the Goddess of Love, Beauty and Sex, encounters Diana, the Roman virgin Goddess of Childbirth, each with weapons raised to the other, with Venus holding a spear and Diana pulling back a bow, arrow poised.

Symbolising the struggle of the soul in terms of the turmoil between love's desire and chastity's abstinence, Diana is joined in her fight by her Nymph escorts and Pallas, the daughter of Triton, against Satyrs and predacious male Gods prominent in mythological tales of love.

As her son Cupid watches over the ensuing battle, Venus is portrayed in a suggestive pose, her only clothing that of a sash wrapped around her waist, its blue colouring represented in ancient Roman times as the sexual indulgence of the carnal wants of the wearer.

THE CANTERBURY TALES
THE SECOND NUN'S TALE
GEOFFREY CHAUCER

It would be Geoffrey Chaucer's telling of the Second Nun's Tale that would bring the virtue of Chastity to light in his fourteenth century parable of the sins and virtues as seen under the Christian Church in his work of The Canterbury Tales.

With pilgrims exchanging stories of sin and virtue on their long pilgrimage it comes to the nun of their party to entertain her fellow companions.

Endowed with great shyness and modesty, the nun begins her tale of chastity much to the attention of all those seated around her.

Telling of a young noble woman of Rome, Cecilia, who was noted for her unique singing voice and aptitude to music, the nun explains how in Cecilia's love and devotion for the Virgin Mary, Cecilia herself vows to keep her virginity and remain in the act of chastity for the rest of her life.

Being of noble birth and destined to marry, Cecilia is betrothed to the handsome young man Valerian. On their wedding night Cecilia decrees her chastity in telling her new husband that should anyone violate her body they will be slain by her Guardian Angel.

Asking to see the angel, Valerian is told that he must first be baptised by Pope Urban. It is on being baptised that Valerian sees the angel and is granted one wish, of which he takes in wishing for his brother to be baptised also.

The nun continues with her story and speaks of the martyrdom of Cecilia for her beliefs and chaste lifestyle.

Although answering her accusers with great intelligence in defending her faith, Cecilia was still condemned to death.

First being lowered into boiling water, Cecilia survives her ordeal brought about from her belief in God and goes on to also survive the three strikes given across her neck by an executioner's sword.

Living for three more days, Cecilia finally succumbs to death. This prompts Pope Urban to venerate Cecilia, and so the martyr of chastity became St. Cecelia, the patron of singing, musicians and poets.

THE SECOND DEADLY SIN

GLUTTONY

Noun: gluttony / ˈɡlʌt(ə)ni/
Habitual greed or excess in life's pleasures
"Obesity is a sign of gluttony in most cases."
Synonyms: greed, greediness, overeating, overconsumption, binge eating, gluttonousness, voraciousness, wolfishness.

'He hath eaten me out of house and home; he hath put all my substance into that fat belly of his.'

Henry IV, Mistress Quickly speaking of Falstaff
William Shakespeare

An Introduction to Gluttony

Closely associated with the deadly sin of avarice, the common perception of gluttony is in the overindulgence of food and drink, of which such consumption it taken to the extreme. Through history it is gluttony's relationships with over eating and the taking of alcohol to excess that has forged this identification.

This can be seen in the literature depicting ancient Rome, where it was not unusual for those in a position to do so to eat and drink to their heart's content until surpassing the body's capacity to hold any more, only to then vomit what had been consumed and so be able to start eating and drinking again.

There are examples of these actions in different cultures across the world, but there are other facets of gluttony than that of an over consumption of food and drink. Gluttony can be found within the overindulgence of anything which gives an individual pleasure.

In Hinduism, scripture has its moments of gluttony when a student focuses on too much study and so loses the ability to see the world around them and what is present in their own life, and in the Catholic Church an overriding joy in the presence of another soul presents itself as a gluttonous act. This occurs when a person wants more and more time with the individual they are so intently focused upon, carried with the lack of understanding that said person may not have the same ability as them for the company of others.

Another form of gluttony is that of Delicacy, a state within the Church that is viewed as a person demanding their own way. This category of gluttony houses the subtle emotional manipulation of others to get what is wanted to a degree which surpasses the norm.

These manifestations of gluttony in history have carried through into modern day. It is not uncommon for doctors of the western world to diagnose that a main reason behind the rise of obesity today is not down to the high sugar levels and fats in food but to gluttony, of which a little temperance wouldn't go amiss now and again. More evidence of gluttony in the west concerns the acts of shopping, where hoards can be seen on the high streets laden with numerous bags filled with newly bought clothes, most of which may never be worn. These examples are an indication that the age old sin of gluttony is still at play amongst those who don't know when to say enough is enough.

GLUTTONY IN RELIGION

CHRISTIANITY

'Be not among drunkards or among gluttonous eaters of meat, for the drunkard and the glutton will come to poverty, and slumber will clothe them with rags.'
Proverbs 23: 20-21

Gluttony is regarded in Christianity as a sin of withholding food from those who have little in means of sustenance.

Taken from the Latin 'gluttire' and implying a love for the over consumption of amenities, these comforts include those of wealth and material gains as much as food and drink, all of which are also seen as strategies of gluttony which lead to the extravagant needs of a believer suffering from the sin.

Observed in the eyes of God, gluttony is a means of testing an individual so they may reach out to temperance in overcoming the temptation of excess.

'They tested god in their heart by demanding the food they craved.'
Psalms 78: 18

The Catholic Church's views on gluttony is that there are various forms in which the sin can take shape in a believer, each of which are concerned with the aspects of delight and can be equated in a similar vein as the disparate wants of food and drink.

These actions can be depicted as the need for that extra little bit more pleasure from something, or somebody, than it or they were conceived to give.

In terms of focus, this aspect of gluttony becomes apparent when an individual focuses on one thing, one single pleasure. This leads to developing into a problem when the ability to enjoy other delights comes into play, leaving said believer with an insatiable desire for one thing and one thing only, resulting in their pleasure ultimately overriding their chosen joy's capabilities.

Another type of gluttony takes the form of demanding too much of others, albeit emotionally or in the wanting of another's time that supersedes an individual's own perception of company.

The demanding of too much of people also plays a role in that of demanding another's time. This only leads to anguish within the glutton as their expectations of others are rarely achieved, so leaving the sufferer of gluttony detached and unfulfilled.

There is another category of gluttony that's subtle behaviours are often masked behind a passive exterior. This is seen as the act of delicacy and can be described as the practice of an individual wanting things their own way.

The gluttony hidden within the emotional manipulation of another's nature into receiving what is wanted sees the sin of gluttony at its worst, for the actions of excess in pleasures, be they of food or other forms of desires, pale in comparison of the deceitfulness in which a glutton may employ in order to get what they want; to get their own was with no consideration for another's views or feelings.

This dishonesty is carried out regularly amongst the interactions of friendships, romantic relationships and in the work place. Often supported by using guilt towards another to influence an outcome towards what is desired, the Church regards these activities of emotional manoeuvres as the revealing of gluttony's true selfish standing within the seven deadly sins.

BUDDHISM

'When a person is constantly mindful, and knows when enough food has been taken, all their afflictions become more slender.'
Gautama Buddha

In Buddhist doctrine, gluttony is viewed as a mental state that leads to a clouding of the mind which in turn manifests into the objectionable actions named Kleshas.

The Kleshas include elements of the emotions described amongst others in being destructive, negative and disturbing. In the Mahayana Tibetan tradition of Buddhism there are around fifty five Kleshas included in the Mahayana Mahaparinirvana Sutra, ranging from deceit, pride and wrong livelihood to attachment, ill will and gluttony. These are regarded as being states of mind to avoid in order for the soul to ultimately reach Nirvana so it may escape the endless cycle of reincarnation and suffering in the world.

A form of avoidance of gluttonous ways in Buddhism is performed in the action of fasting.

In the Theravada branch of Buddhism that is predominant throughout South East Asia, fasting is carried out by the majority of Buddhist monks and nuns following the Vinaya which are a set of rules passed down by Buddha onto his disciples.

Although these rules differ little from the concepts of Tibetan Buddhism, there are some minor differences which are as varied as the discrepancies of yawning or of whistling.

In the act of fasting, it is not uncommon for a Buddhist monk or nun to not eat after their noon time meal. This is regarded as leaving the body and mind clear with no added weight of food to give the consciousness a certain heaviness and so aid in the practice of meditation.

An extension of avoiding gluttony through ways of mediation centres on the practitioner refraining from food altogether for days at a time, yet this practice is only carried out by those experienced in the act and cultivation of medative proficiency.

HINDUISM

'Even nectar is poison if taken to excess.'
Hindu Proverb

The theology of Hinduism states that in eating with gluttonous intent the food which gives energy to the individual's body is instead taken away in the act overindulgence, leaving the mind and body overloaded in the excess of its desire to consume more.

A pursuit for intellectual wisdom and knowledge is also viewed in much the same way. In the goal to explore a spiritual path through scripture a student may become focused on such matters to a degree that emphasis is lost on other things in their life. As with the overconsumption of food the mind loses energy also and instead becomes heavy in an overload of 'too much thought'.

Although not part of the Arishapvarga – the six passions of lust, anger, greed, attachment, pride, and jealousy, the advocates of gluttony are challenged to find their way out of the sin and to achieve Moksha, the term used in Hindu philosophy for the eventual liberation of the soul and the freedom of attaining self-realisation of mind.

SIKHISM

'The world is deceived and polluted by riches, youth and egotism.'
Guru Granth Sahib

As one of Sikhism's five weaknesses of the soul's spiritual essence, aspects of gluttony are found within greed (Lobh) in Sikh terminology.

Alongside Kaam (lust), Krodh (rage), Ahankar (pride) and Moha (attachment), greed is classed as one of the 'Five Thieves' or 'Panj Dosh'.

In the aim of attaining dominance over these five characteristics of the human condition, a Sikh must not let the influence of one of these vices to enter their thoughts or become an aspect of daily life.

Observed as being auspicious, the number five is used in the Five Thieves in significance to the five faces of Shiva, the five rivers of the Punjab, the Sutlej, Beas, Ravi, Chenab and Jhelum, which are all tributaries of the sacred Indus River and give the Punjab - translated as 'Land of Five Rivers' its name. The number five also goes on to symbolise the five moral precepts of Buddha and the vows found in Jainism.

As a Sikh searches for God both internally and externally in the world and in the environment in which they live, it is of the upmost importance to find such unity by abstaining from the vices found in the theology of the Five Thieves and not submitting to the temptations held on offer.

GLUTTONY IN MYTHOLOGY

GREEK

The Greek Goddess and personification of Gluttonous ways, Adephagia lived in her temple home on the island of Sicily.

Worshiped as for reasons for a bountiful harvest in agricultural terms, it would be her overindulgence with food which gave reason for such veneration within the ancient Greek farming communities.

Closely linked to Adephagia's joys of consumption, son of Zeus and Semele, Dionysus the Greek God of Wine making and Religious ecstasy is also associated with the sin of gluttony.

The last of the Gods to enter Mount Olympus and the only God to have been admitted with a mortal mother, Dionysus portrayed the gluttonous acts of excess concerning wine and alcoholic spirits.

This form of gluttony in not knowing when to stop wanting more still continues today as it has throughout humanities existence, all under Dionysus' watchful contemplations.

ROMAN

Bacchus and Liber, where seen as the Romanized equivalent of Dionysus and held the same attributes as their Greek opposite.

With the image of Bacchus immortalised in Caravaggio's 1595 Baroque painting of the same name, the depiction of the Roman God in his youth, draped in a loose white robe and crowned with a head of grapes and vine leaves, presents the act of gluttony to its onlooker in the half filled goblet of wine that Bacchus calls his observers to join with him and drink from, yet it would be Liber's overtones of drunkenness and freedom of speech which established his connection with Dionysus' excess of gluttony therein produced.

Liber and his female embodiment, the Goddess of Wine, Fertility and Freedom, Liberia, would be celebrated in the springtime festival of The Liberalia, where this ancient Italian ceremony saw to a male boy's passage into manhood through the celebrations of not only offerings towards Liber and Liberia but also in the assemble of a huge feast which included the consumption of large quantities of wine.

GLUTTONY IN ART AND LITERATURE

THE BEETHOVEN FRIEZE, GUSTAV KLIMT

Painted at the dawn of the twentieth century on the wall of the Secession Building, Vienna, Austria, Klimt's seven foot by one hundred and twelve foot 'The Beethoven Frieze' unifies the sin of lust with that of gluttony.

Created by Klimt only for exhibition purposes, it was decided that the painting should remain and is still displayed in the building where it was originally painted today.

Symbolising humanity's want for happiness in a world filled with suffering, the piece depicts gluttony towards the centre of the work as an overweight brunette woman. Half naked from the waist up, her portly figure implies an overindulgence towards food.

In a standing position the brunette is overseen by two beautiful naked women sitting high up behind her, their lithe naked bodies magnifying gluttony's hefty form.

Signifying the unchaste and lust, whilst the blonde woman sits with eyes closed in impure abandonment, the redheaded woman stares provocatively at the painting's viewer.

THE THIEF, THE COOK, HIS WIFE AND HER LOVER PETER GREENAWAY

In Peter Greenaway's 1989 film 'The Cook, the Thief, His Wife & Her Lover', the sin of gluttony is conveyed in the wanton excess of the story's main character Albert Spica.

An English gangster whose nocturnal visits to his newly acquired high class Le Hollandai Restaurant, Spica, played by Michael Gambon, portrays a man whose insatiable wants and acts of egocentric behaviour represents an individual lost in the depths of gluttony, whilst remaining blissfully unaware of the depths to which the sin has placed him in.

In seeing her husband so polluted by gluttony, Spica's wife, Georgina, played by Helen Mirren, finds solace in the love of a regular customer of her husband's restaurant, a kindly bookshop owner.

Their affair is hidden from Spica in the aid of the staff of Le Hollandai, they too as disgusted by the man as his wife, yet the romance is doomed when Spica learns of the affair and has his wife's lover killed by force-feeding him pages from his beloved books.

When Georgina discovers her dead lover she begs the restaurant's head chef to cook the body. The chef agrees and in the films finale the body is set out in the centre of a table laden with delicacies whereupon, overcome with grief, Georgina forces her husband to eat a mouthful of her deceased lover's body.

Finally submitting to his wife's wishes, Spica begins to eat only for Georgina to eventually shoot her husband dead.

Written and directed by Greenaway, the film is shot in a lavish cinematography style evoking that of Renaissance paintings. With darkened backdrops and displays of visual extremes from tables over flowing with rich sumptuous dishes of food to the advocacy of violence and sex, The Cook, the Thief, His Wife & Her Lover shows the effects of gluttony on an individual who has it all in material terms yet wants more just for the sake of it.

DUNE
FRANK HERBERT

Published in 1965, Frank Herbert's science fiction novel Dune portrays gluttony in subtle overtones throughout the epic saga of warring households.

Set in the year 10,191, where planetary systems do battle over the planet Arrakis due to its exclusivity of the treasured spice Melange, acts of gluttony are portrayed in the want of each house for more, so adding to the riches of wealth and power already held.

This is no more evident in that of the House Harkonnen whose deplorable dictator, the Baron Harkonnen, revels in the sin of gluttony.

Rejoicing in his gluttonous ways, the Baron's overindulgence of food has rendered him unable to walk leaving his only option of mobility in the anti-gravity generators sewn into his clothing. Yet even with his intemperance of food, the Baron's gluttony devours another aspect of the sin, in that his desire for gratification for inflicting pain on others is far reaching the needs of satisfaction and he continues his sadistic acts with unlimited delight, not realising his joy in the suffering of another has already been sated.

In the Baron Harkonnen's elations it can be said that his endless display of gluttony is an exaggeration of the sin within the other houses of the Dune universe.

This is shown in the House Corrin, home of Shadam IV, Emperor of the Known Universe, whose want for more power and domination represents gluttony in as much as his desires in wanting more than the lavish assets already held within his house.

THE CANTERBURY TALES: THE PARDONER'S TALE GEOFFREY CHAUCER

The fourteenth of a collection of twenty-four stories within Geoffrey Chaucer's late fourteenth century work of The Canterbury Tales, The Pardoner's Tale is a moral story played out within the theme of gluttony.

As three young men display their gluttony in drinking, gambling and swearing in a tavern, the sounds of a nearby church bell signals the burial of one of their friends who has been killed by a 'privee theef' who is more commonly known as being Death.

Deciding in seeking revenge against Death, the young men agree to go out into the night and kill the one who has seen to the demise of their friend. Asking an old man where they can find their victim, it is explained to them that Death can be found sitting at the base of an old oak tree.

On reaching the tree the three men find a hoard of gold coins and immediately forget about their act of vengeance and decide on sleeping overnight under the tree so they may carry the found coins back to their homes in the morning.

In need of sustenance, the men draw straws as to who will fetch food and wine to see them through the night. When the youngest of the three draws the shortest straw he sets off to retrieve their provisions only for the remaining two to plot to kill him on his return so they may have his share of treasure. Unbeknown to the two, the youngest of the men has had a similar idea and on purchasing food and wine he laces the wine with rat poison.

On his return he is killed by the two men who then, in their celebrations of having more gold coins than before, drink the wine only to be poisoned and so join their youngest friend in death.

THE SECOND HEAVENLY VIRTUE

TEMPERANCE

Noun: temperance / 'tɛmp(ə)r(ə)ns/
Taking moderation in life's pleasures.
"The vicar was a strict advocate of temperance."
Synonyms: abstinence, abstention, sobriety,
restraint, sacrifice, self-control, self-discipline.

'The ingredients of health and long life are great temperance, open air, easy labour, and little care.'

Sir Philip Sidney

AN INTRODUCTION TO TEMPERANCE

The properties of Temperance take many forms and are vital in the development and improvement of an individual's spiritual path.

In world religions, temperance is regarded as one of the most important virtues and is seen as the act of practicing self-control over the wants and desires of the soul in order of achieving joy and peace within an individual's heart and mind.

Theology states that in refraining from the overindulgence of earthly delights in either physical, material or sensual forms a devotee may then achieve advancement to God or other Deities they believe.

Within Buddhist principles it is said that by attaining temperance in a soul's daily life will lead to Nirvana, where suffering of humanity is abolished, and within the Christian Church it is believed that in avoiding temptation and so achieving temperance in a follower's life then they are gaining entrance into the Kingdom of God.

Throughout history temperance can be found in literature denoting the qualities held in mastering the impulses of a want for over consumption.

Plato was a firm believer in the values of temperance. This contributed to the virtue's popularity in ancient Greece and was utilised as a theme in his dialogue of the Charmides, when Socrates speaks of Sophrosyne, the Greek Deity of Self-control and Restraint.

The view Plato held that having a temperate nature was one of the several core morals of an ideal society were agreed upon by Aristotle who said of temperance:

'Temperance and bravery, then, are raided by excess and deficiency'
Aristotle

Over two millennia later, Christianity would abide by the words of ancient Greece's philosophers by forming 'Temperance Movements', where society's over excesses of alcohol was looked on with great distaste.

In advancement of these Christian movements, the Catholic Church would form their own way of tackling the over consumption of alcohol in the 'Teetotal Abstinence Society'.

Both of these movements would go on to influence the drinking habits of millions for over two decades of the twentieth century

TEMPERANCE IN RELIGION

CHRISTIANITY

'Gentleness, self-control; against such things there is no law.'
Galatians 5: 23

Temperance and its values are strengthened in a congregation's conscious beliefs by being included in the Ten Commandments. Temperance's values are portrayed in the seventh Commandment of 'Thou shall not commit adultery' and in the tenth as 'Thou shall not covet thy neighbour's wife'.

As stated, temperance in the commandments is connected to that of the abstinence of sexual relations, yet it would be in the early nineteenth century when the virtues of temperance were put to use in another way.

Viewed as a downfall of society, the consumption of alcoholic spirits in 1820's Britain was looked upon with distain by the Christian Church.

As Britain reached the 1830's a number of Temperance Movements were formed to combat the rise of alcoholism present within the country. These groups and their prudence were to hold great influence over society with similar movements formed during this time in America and the British colonies of Australia and New Zealand.

To tackle the problems of the overindulgence of alcohol, the Catholic Church also formed its own movement. Unlike the Christian Church's outlook that wine and ale were not to be frowned upon, the Catholic view of temperance saw to it that no alcohol was to be consumed, which gave rise to the 'Teetotal Abstinence Society'.

These 'Societies' soon grew in size, most notably in America where fountains were provided throughout the country in parks and recreational areas for citizens to freely drink fresh water and in the development of numerous 'coffee palaces' which too saw the demise of alcohol consumption.

It would be one hundred years later after the forming of these movements and societies that abstinence's popularity began to decline.

The revoking of prohibition laws across America in the mid

1930's saw to the once harsh views of alcohol's pleasures easing within the community and by the end of the Second World War, Britain soon followed the trend.

Today there still remains some traces of temperance towards alcohol. These views are held not in the total abstinence of alcoholic spirits but in the carrying out a degree of self-control in the consumption of alcohol.

BUDDHISM

'Temperance is a tree which as for its root very little contentment, and for its fruit calm and peace.'
Gautama Buddha

In the Buddhist concepts of suffering, the causes of suffering and a soul's escape from suffering, the Four Noble Truths lead a devotee towards the Eight Fold Path which is seen as a guideline for the correct way of living. These Four Noble Truths are:

Dukkha – The truth of suffering.
Samudata – the initiation of Dukkha and the truth of the cause of suffering.
Nirodha – the cessation of Dukkha and the truth of the end of suffering.
Magga – liberation from Dukkha and the truth of the path that frees us from suffering.

The afore mentioned path in Buddha's fourth truth of Magga, tells of the Noble Eight Fold Path, in which the third and fifth precepts speak of the virtue of temperance.

Symbolised by the Dharma (teaching) wheel, its eight spokes represent the eight values of the Noble Path with each step viewed as progress for an individual's soul. When each of these stages are adhered to only then may a soul escape Samsara's circle of life, death and rebirth, and so reach the realm of Nirvana where suffering no longer prevails.

In the Sama Vaca, the third concept of the Eight Fold Path, the actions of right speech are presented in the form of speaking only with compassion for others, of using only uplifting words with no rudeness or connotations of harmful communication.

These acts of correct speech are observed as practicing temperance in an individual's life, as are the ideals found on the Path's fifth precept.

Within the doctrine of the Eight Fold Path's fifth instruction Sama Ajiva, the codes of conduct denote that a devotee of the Buddha must have the right livelihood.

The values of holding the right livelihood are found in working only for that which sustains the devotee and his family, and the avoidance of livelihoods which causes harm to others. These injurious occupations are interpreted as warmongering and in making the deceitful gains of another's money or possessions.

HINDUISM

'Consciousness never occurs for one who eats too much or one who eats too little, nor also for one who sleeps too much or sleeps too little.'
The Bhagavad Gita

Temperance in the actions of self-restraint and self-control are regarded as one of Hinduism's six central virtues.

Observed under the heading of Dama, the concept of which parallels that of having a temperate disposition, is classed as one of the three traits of an individual's personality along with Daana, equating to charity and the deed of giving to others, and Daya, holding a love for all living entities, be them humankind or of the animal kingdom.

The Hindu veneration of the cow is also a show of respect towards Ashima, the premise that all sentient beings have an element of divine spiritual energy within them, which leads the cow to be regarded as the principal epitome of temperance in Hinduism.

Considered as being the greatest gift to another throughout India's rural communities, the cow signifies its temperate disposition through its unconscious acts of endurance, strength and selfless amenity to humanity.

According to Hindu theology Dama can be reached within all individuals by adhering to five principals of self-control. These are seen as refraining from greed, not instigating deceit, theft of another's property, the misconduct of extra marital affairs, and the promoting or participating in violence acts.

It is also viewed that by practicing and cultivating temperance in life is a step towards generating good Karma in this lifetime and in subsequent lifetimes to follow.

SIKHISM

'Practice truth, contentment and kindness; this is the most excellent way of life.'
Guru Granth Sahib

Sikhism's five virtues are seen as the antidote to its polar opposite of the five evils.

With the virtue of Sat calling upon the qualities of truth, Daya that of compassion, Nimrata being the practice of humility and Pyaar of love, Santokh is the embodiment of contentment within the soul that can be reached if the five evils of envy, wrath, avarice and jealousy are eliminated from a followers life.

'One who is so blessed by the formless Lord God renounces selfishness, and becomes the dust of all.'
Guru Granth Sahib

By cultivating temperance in life the rewards found in Santokh's release can be attained. As is with the remaining four virtues in Sikhism, by applying temperance to each facet within an individual's life leads to freedom from the five evils.

TEMPERANCE IN MYTHOLOGY

GREEK

The personified spirit of moderation and restraint, Sophrosyne is viewed as representing temperance in ancient Greek mythology.

The opposite of hubris, a state of pride and over confidence verging on arrogance, Sophrosyne was one of the spirits to escape Pandora's box when it was opened by Pandora, the world's first mortal woman, fashioned in clay by the Gods and bestowed with beauty from Aphrodite and given the gift of cunning by Hermes,

Sophrosyne then abandoned humankind and returned to Mount Olympus.

Imbued with self-knowledge, Sophrosyne's qualities were cited as being the ideal traits a character should possess. This coupled with the abilities of self-control and prudence in life's pleasures led to the great respect shown by the ancient Greeks, with examples of her virtues told in homer's The Iliad and likened to a Divine Goddess by the playwright Euripides.

ROMAN

The Roman mythological representation of the Greek spirit Sophrosyne, Continentia, took the mantle of depicting temperance in ancient Rome.

As with her counterpart Sophrosyne, Continentia too held the values of moderation and forethought and was venerated for her excellence of character in restraint of earthly desires.

Observed that by following her values then an individual would therefore receive peace, harmony and joy in their lives. Continentia's virtues would go to be included in 'The Oracle of Delphi' with the sayings of 'Know thy self' and 'Nothing in excess'.

In the Roman and Greek philosophy of the time, it was believed that in living a simple life with good intentions that health and happiness would be the reward. These thoughts would prompt the Roman poet Juena to award the moniker to both Sophrosyne's and Continentia's values with the words 'healthy mind, healthy body'.

So influential was Continentia that her bodily image would often be reproduced on the sides of wine urns and pottery drinking vessels, reminding partakers of her thoughts on overindulgence

TEMPERANCE IN ART AND LITERATURE

THE GIRLHOOD OF MARY VIRGIN
DANTE GABRIEL ROSSETTI

Born in London in 1828, Dante Gabriel Rossetti the English poet and painter would complete his painting 'The Girlhood of Mary Virgin' one year after the founding of the Pre-Raphaelite Brotherhood alongside his contemporaries William Holman Hunt and John Everett Millais in 1848.

Seeing the Virgin Mary as the epitome of female virtues, with a backdrop of the Sea of Galilee, his painting shows Mary as a girl with her mother Saint Anne and her father Saint Joachim in a garden, all watched over by an angel.

The Girlhood of Mary Virgin is filled with rich symbolism throughout the piece with lilies denoting purity, grape vines of truth, a dove for the Holy Spirit sitting above a lamp signifying devotion, and a rose representing virginity. The future event of the Passion of Christ is also suggested in the red draping of material and in the form of a crucifix in the guise of trellising behind Saint Anne.

As the angel watches over Mary and her mother she rests her hand on six books piled high on the floor. Rossetti included these different coloured books as to represent the Church's three theological virtues of blue for Faith, green for Hope and gold for Charity, beneath of which are three of the four cardinal virtues, these being, brown for Diligence, beige for Discretion and white to depict Temperance. With Rossetti's mother modelling for Saint Anne and his sister Christina as Mary, Rossetti would explain the symbolism within The Girlhood of Mary Virgin through the words of two sonnets which are now written on the frame of his painting.

ALLEGORY OF TEMPERANCE
LUCA GIORDANO

Commissioned to create a group of ten ornate oil studies for fresco and ceiling reliefs for the Palazzo Medici Riccardi in Florence, Italy, Giordano's early 1680's Allegory of Temperance features several people standing or seated around an elephant and a dolphin in the near centre of the painting.

Floating above them are three robust women representing Youth, Tranquillity and Voluptuous, and three Seraphim before a background of stormy dark blue skies, bringing the lightness portrayed in these hovering figures to life.

Three of the grounded figures are allegories of the sins of Sloth, Envy and Hunger, whereas those remaining symbolise the Cardinal virtues of Modesty shown receiving flowers, Sobriety with a key in one hand while her foot rests on a dolphin's head, and Temperance stands high above an elephant holding a clock and a bridal.

THE DIVINE COMEDY: PARADISO, DANTE ALIGHIERI

In Paradiso, the third and final part of Dante Alighieri's epic saga The Divine Comedy, Dante is guided through the realms of Heaven by Beatrice, the personification of Theology and of the Beatific vision, which encapsulates the ultimate direct self communication with God towards an individual.

As Dante and Beatrice leave the Garden of Eden at the summit of Mount Purgatory, they ascend through the fires separating the earth and the moon where then Beatrice explains that Heaven consists of nine celestial spheres in which together they shall travel and meet with several blessed souls, telling Dante that these spheres of Heaven begin with the Moon and continue outwards through Mercury, Venus, the Sun, Mars, Jupiter, Saturn, the stars and the Primum Mobile, the outermost sphere that gives Heaven's other spheres motion.

As they travel through the first six spheres, Dante and Beatrice arrive at Saturn, where they encounter Saint Peter Damian, the allegory of Temperance.

It is within the domain of Heaven's seventh sphere that Saint Peter, the former Benedictine monk and Cardinal of 11th century Italy, gives Dante an insight into the virtue and values of temperance by expressing the need of forgoing lavish riches and material goods in order to live a lifetime of temperate means.

With Beatrice at his side, Dante listens to Saint Peter's words and begins to understand the need for practicing temperance by living a moral and honourable life, and by avoiding humanity's sometimes desire for overindulgence and excess in life's pleasures.

BRAVE NEW WORLD ALDOUS HUXLEY

In Aldous Huxley's 1932 novel depicting a futuristic totalitarian utopian society, it would be the lack of Temperance held within civilisation's excess of the pleasures of technology, sex and psychological manipulation that would leave the novel's protagonist John, tormented by the absence of morality in those around him.

Set in London in 2540 AD, humanity is now created by genetic engineering where each new-born's life is predestined, leaving those not chosen to lead the privileged life as an Alpha to become an Epsilon. Genetically produced to have a lower intelligence and destined for a lifetime of work, an Epsilon's work is paid in their only delight in life, the happiness inducing drug soma.

When Bernard Marx, an Alpha member of society visits an reservation of 'savages', so called because it's community has been left without the advancements of technology and where humanity still reproduces normally, he meets a young 'savage' man named John and decides to bring him back to 'civilization'.

On his arrival to London, John's temperate nature is viewed as being that of a savage by society, yet through their fascination towards this man of good morals he becomes a celebrity.

Shown the ways of his new environment where the processes of sleep learning and casual sex are played out by the Alphas to the degrees of great overindulgence, John eventually turns his back on the anti-emotional civilisation to which he has been introduced and finds work as a lighthouse guard so he may live the temperate life lost within those he now lives amongst.

The Third Deadly Sin

AVARICE

Noun: avarice / 'av(ə)rɪs/
Extreme greed for wealth or material gain.
"He was rich beyond the dreams of avarice."
Synonyms: greed, acquisitiveness, cupidity,
Covetousness, avariciousness, rapacity,
rapaciousness, graspingness, materialism.

'He who is contented with what he has, would not be content with what he would like to have.'

Socrates

An Introduction to Avarice

The sin of Avarice is seen not only as an immorality of the wealthy but is equally perceived as a temptation for those with little in way of possessions, portrayed by an endless want for money and belongings beyond their means.

Classed as a sin of desire alongside lust and gluttony, avarice can be employed in other practices far reaching the need for money, where the hoarding of material possessions or the manipulation of others by way of betrayal or disloyalty can also be seen as greed, no more so than when these misdeeds are used for emotional gain.

These acts of avarice were brought to light in the words of Dante, when offenders of avarice were laid face down to the ground in purgatory, their hands tied behind them as a result of a lifetime spent focused only on earthly desires, and it would be in the late 19th century when the English Roman Catholic Archbishop of Westminster, Henry Edward Manning said 'avarice plunges a man deep into the mire of his world, so that he makes it to be his God.'

In many world religions avarice is observed as a vice. From the Buddhist belief of 'The Three Poisons' to the Hindu identification of greed as written in the ancient epic 'The Mahabharata', each culture and tradition has its own identification of the wrongs of avarice.

Instilling the strong craving to gain, greed can lead to the illusion of self-sufficiency in the possessions gained often at the cost of another. As comfort for the soul is seen in the attaining of a desired item, be it a larger home, person or monies, the security once thought to be contained within that want soon slips away, only to be replaced by the need for another item. And so the individual's endless quest for peace of mind continues its cycle of wishes and desires.

In identifying these wants only then can avarice be denied. By internalising the actions that drive us towards greed and the manipulations sometimes carried forth in which to get what we want, we can start to see the reasoning behind our actions. Is it always necessary to have more possessions than another so we may look more successful in their eyes? Is it required to have bank balances which surpass more than we can possibly spend in order to indicate how good a person we must be? By way of self-analysis in our everyday undertakings the complexities of how avarice affects our lives reveals the illusory implications of our wants and needs.

AVARICE IN RELIGION

BUDDHISM

'On life's journey faith is nourishment. Virtuous deeds are a shelter. Wisdom is the light by day and right mindfulness is the protection by night. If a man lives a pure life nothing can destroy him. If he has conquered greed nothing can limit his freedom.'
Gautama Buddha

Lobha, the ancient Sanskrit word for greed, is often defined in Buddhist literature as the want for something we think will fulfil us, which in turn only produces suffering in our lives when our needs are not satisfied.

These wants and desires are considered to run throughout humanity's existence and are shown in Buddhist scripture under the guise of 'The Three Poisons', Lobha - greed, Moha - ignorance and Dvesha - hatred.

Known also as 'The Three Unwholesome Roots', or 'The Roots of Unhappiness' in some Mahayana and Theravada Buddhist scriptures, The Three Poisons are represented by three creatures, with Lobha shown as a cockerel, Moha a pig and Dvesha as a snake.

Called the Akusala-Mula in Sanskrit, this translates as Akusala meaning evil and Mula meaning root, and so the Three Poisons are said to represent the root of all evil from where all damaging actions come.

These Three Poisons can be seen pictured within Buddhist paintings of The Wheel of Life adorning the walls of the majority of temples and shrines in Tibet, Bhutan, Nepal and northern India.

Also going under the name of Bhavachakra, The Wheel of Life depicts a large spinning eight spoke wheel representing the world of Samsara, where all humankind wanders aimlessly within the constant karmic cycles of life, death and rebirth. It was this wandering world of Samsara that the Buddha eventually left when gaining enlightenment, and is the place all Buddhists strive to escape also.

The Three Poisons of cockerel, pig and snake can be found depicted in the center of Samsara within the Wheel of Life's hub.

Placed in a circular state chasing the other's tail, it is the energy of these three creatures that gives the wheel it momentum which promotes Samsara's continuous rotation of reincarnation for those yet to reach the enlightenment.

Greed can also be represented in Buddhism through the act of attachment, where those caught within the sin grasp at what they have in fear of losing that so precious to them. It is in this act that the trepidation of leaving what theirs is behind produces great anxiety and so leads to the state of suffering in said individual.

One of the many reasons behind the use of the Three Poisons within the Wheel of Life is for the Buddhist devotee to question themselves if they are at a loss as to why they may be experiencing any negative emotions. This is achieved by questioning if it is the representation of the cockerel, the pig or the snake which are making them feel that way?

CHRISTIANITY

'Having lost all sensitivity, they have given themselves over to sensuality so as to indulge in every kind of impurity, with a continual lust for more.'
Ephesians 4: 19

Seen in the Christian church as the inordinate love of having possessions or riches, it is recognised that the primary concern of avarice is that it pulls us away from God, as it was He on building the earth who provided us with all we need.

Isolation is also seen as a consequence of avarice within the Church. With a need for additional riches and possessions we must give something up to make space for our newly found riches or assets. This is often demonstrated in the abandonment of others in an individual's want for more, where focus becomes purely on the self, and so producing a total neglect for the needs of another.

These aspects of avarice would be confirmed in the words of the thirteenth century Italian Dominican friar St. Thomas Aquinas, who said avarice to be 'a sin against God, inasmuch as man contemns things eternal for the sake of temporal things.'

Often symbolised by a frog, in Catholicism avarice is classed as a mortal sin that 'kills the life of sanctifying grace.' Viewed as an introduction towards breaking one or more of the Ten Commandments, the price paid for committing the sin of avarice is high, with its sinner destined to boil in a vat of hot oil for eternity.

As Christianity's perception of avarice expanded through the Middle Ages and into modern day it was no longer seen as a sin preoccupied only with the acquisition of material goods.

As time progressed within the Church, it soon became identified that the actions of the emotional manipulation of others, either by way of guilt or victimhood, was becoming an apparent characteristic of avarice.

Commonly performed in relationships, be they family, friendship or romantic, Christianity acknowledged how greed has evolved within humankind, shown in present day times with an individual's tendency of collecting people as a sign of status. Another unsightly aspect of modern day avarice is often found in the corporate world where the using of another in order to gain advantage is common, often with the pursuer of wealth deceiving others also prone to greed, those of which who are often seeking the individual's similar quest for emotional security. This is noted in Catholicism as a sense of complacency within which lays a total self-independence from God.

HINDUISM

'Hell has three gates: lust, anger, and greed.'
The Bhagavad Gita

Found within the Hinduism religion, avarice is classified as one of the 'Six Passions' known as the 'Arishadvarga'.

Using a derivative of the Sanskrit word for greed as seen in Buddhism, Lobh is viewed as a negative feature which prevents humanity from attaining salvation, or in Hindu dialects, Moksha. As with other religions, Hinduism identifies avarice by the selfishness of ones actions for personal gains.

The Six Passions are seen as the central creeds of Kali Yuga. Described in Sanskrit scriptures, the Kali Yuga is the age of vice and sited as the last of four stages the world passes through as part of the cycle of Yugas or epochs, of which we in present day are said to be living in. As a prophetic view on greed, it is said of the final Yuga that avarice and wrath will be common and when the ignorance of Dharma (teaching) occurs, humans will openly display animosity towards each other.

Also called one of the Six Evil Passions, Lobh comes forth when the ego has joined forces with Maya, the covetous strength of creation. Alongside the other passions of Lust - Kama, Anger – Crodha, Attachment – Moha, Pride - Ahankar and Jealousy – Matsarya, it is these sins that influence humankind to lose the knowledge of their 'True Being'.

SIKHISM

'The world is deceived and plundered by riches, youth, greed and egotism.'
Guru Granth Sahib

Avarice is specified in Sikh scriptures under the same Hindu name of Lobh, when the Guru Granth Sahib talks of the Five Evils. Similar to the Six Poisons in Hinduism literature, the Five Evils does not include Matsarya – Jealousy.

Lobh is regarded as the powerful yearning for worldly possessions, either riches or belongings of luxury. This belief is coupled with the individual's consistent compulsion to own that of which belongs to another, of which makes the sinner of avarice selfish enough to be diverted from both community and religious obligations specified to them.

Although within Sikhism it is not deemed wrong to be wealthy or looked up to by another, failings in the acts of greed are seen when the emphasis on riches and material achievements takes focus away from God and said devotee begins to move away from prayer and into the self-centred world of impartiality from spirit.

As with Hinduism, the last stage of Kali Yuga is metaphorically recognised in Sikhism, with emphasis on its devotees to meditate as often as possible so they may reach the state of enlightenment and so resulting in being one with God. This is seen in Guru Granth Sahib's words.

'Now, the Dark Age of Kali Yuga has come.
Plant the Naam, the Name of the One Lord.
It is not the season to plant other seeds.
Do not wander lost in doubt and delusion.'
Guru Granth Sahib

Avarice in Mythology

Greek

Avarice is depicted in different scenarios throughout Greek mythology, most famously in the tale of King Midas of the royal house of Phrygia, whose wish for the ability to turn everything he touched into gold was granted by the God of Fertility and Wine, Dionysus.

Inevitably the King's greed soon became apparent when all he tried to eat and drink turned into gold, leading to avarice's misery to be established when Midas hugged his daughter Philomena, only resulting in his loved one turning to gold also.

With all the myths of avarice's downfalls presented in Greek mythology it was Plutus the Greek God of Wealth whose title would link him most predominantly to the sin.

Son of Demeter the Goddess of Agriculture, Fertility and Harvest and regarded as the 'Devine Child', Plautus literally means wealth in ancient Greek text.

With the significance of Plutus' name, he would become synonymous with the God Pluto ruler of the Underworld, thought to be because of the rich wealth of minerals and precious ores found beneath the earth's surface.

This would lead to the English nouns of 'Plutolatry' – the reverence and excessive devotion to wealth, and 'Plutocrat' – an individual who rules by the advantage of wealth.

Roman

Accounted in classical Roman script, it would be Minerva the Goddess of Wisdom and Strategy who with the aid of other Gods and Dieties would see to the expulsion of avarice.

Daughter of Jupiter, King of the Gods in ancient Roman religion, and niece of Pluto in Greek and Roman text, Minerva and two other patrons of artistic pursuits, the divine hero Hercules (the Roman name for the Greek divine hero Heracles), and the Olympian deity Apollo, were joined by eight of the nine muses and in a display of solidarity expelled avarice from the Temple of Muses.

This is portrayed in Ugo da Carpi's sixteenth century engraving

"Hercules chasing Avarice from the Temple of the Muses" depicting avarice as the one who is known to cling to material possessions and is fated as the enemy of all creativity.

AVARICE IN ART AND LITERATURE

THE GARDEN OF EARTHLY DELIGHTS
HIERONYMUS BOSCH

The Dutch master Hieronymus Bosch portrayed the seven deadly sins in his most renowned painting 'The Garden of Earthly Delights.'

The triptych in oil paints set on oak panels depicts three scenes of Biblical theology. Viewed from left to right, the left panel illustrates God bestowing Adam and Eve the Garden of Eden, and while the middle square panel shows an array of frolicking animals and nudes accompanied by succulent oversized fruits it is Bosch's right panel that represents the consequences of sin.

Revealing the bane found in damnation, the Hellscape of Bosch's masterpiece stands in stark contrast to its two previous depictions of God's loving grace.

With sinners pictured amongst nightmarish creatures presenting and administrating various heinous tortures to them, each of the seven deadly sins are featured amid the melee of ingenious torments.

It is here that the sin of avarice is presented in the lower half of the right panel, where between a bird headed figure and a man being deceived into giving money to the Church by a pig dressed in a nun's veil, a figure can be seen discarding golden coins for the rest of eternity from his hind quarters into a culvert filled with other offenders of greed.

GREED AND AVARICE. CATS FIGHTING IN A LARDER
PAUL DE VOS

The seventeenth century Flemish Baroque style painter Paul de Vos, was renowned for his depictions of animals, still life and hunting scenes and was a leading figure of the Antwerp painters alongside Rubens and Dyck.

Two of his works would portray the acts of avarice played out in the animal kingdom.

His mid-seventeenth century painting 'Greed and Avarice' shows a master's dog defending his quarry, a large bloodied carcass, from the snarls and want of two other dogs beside him.

Up keeping the animosity held in 'Greed and Avarice', de Vos' painting 'Cats Fighting in a Larder', shows hostility in the actions as two cats watch the brawl of four cats in their want for control of a table laden with goose, pheasant, vegetables and bread, and a stick holding a brace of chaffinches by their heads, of which one cat's paw has already claimed.

SIDDHARTHA
HERMAN HESSE

Released in 1922, Hermann Hesse's novel Siddhartha tells the story of a man of which after the book is named and his journey of self-discovery during the era of the Buddha.

With Siddhartha being Buddha's name also, his full title being that of the Prince of Kapilavastu Siddhartha Gautama, the book documents one man's meeting with the self-same trials and wonders as his counterpart. Leaving his home behind, Siddhartha steps out into the world to become a Sramana, the Pali name for a 'seeker' of spiritual truths. Accompanied by his childhood friend Govinda, Siddhartha relinquishes his possessions, meditates and fasts on his pursuit for enlightenment.

In ancient Sanskrit text, Siddhartha can be translated as siddha – 'the attained' and artha – 'of that which is explored.' When placed together these two words lead on to produce a new phrase, 'the one who has achieved his aim.'

Avarice is featured within Hesse's novel when our protagonist meets with an older merchant by the name of Kamaswami in hope of learning the business ways of trading.

It is through Kamaswami's teachings that Siddhartha learns the happiness sought from possessions is merely an illusion and so steps through such misconceptions to rise above the trappings of avarice.

This is confirmed by Kamaswami's disbelief that his student can retain such happiness without the wealth and worldly goods he himself owns, his misunderstandings defined by Siddhartha's view that money and commerce are just a game that will never lead to full spiritual fulfilment.

PETRARCH

'Five enemies of peace inhabit us – avarice, ambition, envy, anger and pride; if these were to be banished, we should infallibly enjoy perpetual peace.'
Francesco Petrarch

These are the words of fourteenth century cleric and poet Francesco Petrarch. Born in Arezzo, Tuscany, his writing is widely celebrated as being an influence to today's modern Italian language.

A devoted classical scholar and considered the 'Father of Humanism' and 'Father of the Renaissance', his studies would delve deep into the theology of the seven deadly sins.

His ordination as a cleric allowed his passion for writing and ancient literature to be realised, more so aided by his being awarded Rome's poet laureate in 1341, and as a diplomatic envoy for the Roman Catholic Church this also enabled Petrarch to search for long lost classical manuscripts.

It would be during his lifetime of study that the temptations of avarice would not go unnoticed during the Italian province's times of plague, when those around him coveted their possessions and riches.

THE THIRD HEAVENLY VIRTUE

CHARITY

Noun: charity / 'chăr'ĭ-tē)/
The voluntary giving of help.
"The care of the poor must not be left to private charity."
Synonyms: kindness, generosity, aid, welfare, relief, mercy.

'A bone to the dog is not charity. Charity is the bone shared with the dog, when you are just as hungry as the dog.'

Jack London

An Introduction to Charity

Seen as a spiritual antidote to avarice, the heavenly virtue of Charity is also classed as the actions of generosity, kindness and giving.

With charity known as the bestowment of goodwill towards others and the love of all humanity, the sin of avarice and charity are eternally linked through the action of giving. This is revealed in if the giving to another is for reasons of advantage to the beneficiary; the sin of avarice emerges in the cunning betrayal of charity's virtue of giving wholeheartedly and without any want in return.

These traits of the connection and ultimate eradication of greed are written within the scriptures of religions across the world no matter how ancient or new these faiths may be.

An example of such teachings can be found in the traditions of Buddhism, where the act of compassion in which Buddha explains the need for individuals to cultivate the virtue of kindness and generosity, made apparent in the bestowing of alms to those who have taken refuge within their faith and of the selfless acts of giving to those who have little or are in a less fortunate position than ourselves.

Buddhism is closely linked with the other main religions of Asia and South East Asia, with Hinduism also following the virtue of charity in the form of Dana, the Sanskrit word for generosity.

It is of little surprise that these religions share a similar outlook and ethic, as Buddha himself was born within a community steeped in Indian beliefs and philosophies in the Nepalese town of Lumbini in 623 BC.

Within the Christian Church, charity is one of the most fundamental of virtues as to be charitable brings a believer closer to God.

First truly perceived in the Middle Ages by the Church, the act of charity became ever present as the centuries progressed, with deeds of generosity perceived as a cornerstone to the foundations of the Christian faith.

Charity in Religion

Buddhism

'Generosity brings happiness at every stage of its expression. We experience joy in forming the intention to be generous. We experience joy in the actual act of giving something. And we experience joy in remembering the fact that we have given.'
Gautama Buddha

Generosity is revealed throughout the continents of Asia and South East Asia under the Sanskrit title of 'Dana,' by the giving of alms, an act where devotees willing give money, food and drink to Buddhist monks, nuns and people of a high spiritual advancement.

Dating back to the Vedic traditions of India, Dana is closely linked with Asia's major religions of Hinduism, Jainism and Sikhism, as well as being a core belief in the Mahayana and Theravada Buddhist customs where followers of the Buddha are encouraged to cultivate the practice of giving freely.

Dana can take the form of both the giving of money and material goods as well as the act of giving emotional support to another in times of distress. Buddhists believe that the deed of giving without seeking anything in return provides them with not only greater spiritual riches but will also provide them with advancement on their transcendent journey from this life time onto the next.

Regarded as decreasing the desires and urges held within the sin of avarice which eventually leads to continued suffering, generosity is one of the six 'Paramitas' (Perfections) of Buddhism.

The Six Perfections in Mahayana Buddhism are viewed as a guide to the path of enlightenment and the six characteristics inherent to humankind.

With generosity leading the six Paramitas the other are ethics/morality, tolerance/patience, energy/perseverance, meditation and finally wisdom itself.

Acknowledged that an enlightened person holds all six perfections, it is for others to try to attain the same position, the result being in that if we are not enlightened then our path is obscured by one or all of the delusions of greed, anger and fear.

Translated as 'Sbyin Pa' in Tibetan, Dana or generosity is the reaching of giving fully from the self without attachment. This leads to an attitude of non-clinging and is incentive in the action of providing gifts to others.

In Buddhist scripture the motivation of giving with purely selfless intents is called Bodhicitti, and it is stressed that the amount of which is given bears little importance as it is the act which carries such merits.

There are three categories of the perfection of generosity, these being the giving of the material, the gifts of protection from fear to others and the teaching of Buddha's words, known as the Dharma.

Generosity within Buddhism is seen to generate Bodhisattva's greatest virtue of compassion, where the clinging and greed of another's emotions is dispelled from us and so leads us further along our spiritual path towards enlightenment.

As well as furthering ourselves and others in the actions of generosity it is important to develop the practice of giving. Yet in the endeavour of giving comes great responsibility, where questions arise of when and what to give, and what, if any, are the reasons for these gifts for others. Do these gives bestowed come from the heart of selfless actions, or is there a hint of what you may receive from the recipient in return?

CHRISTIANITY

'Do not neglect to show hospitality to strangers,
for thereby some have entertained angels unawares.'
Luke 6: 38

Within Christian theology the word charity is derived from the Latin 'caritas' meaning altruistic love, this word in turn resulted from the Greek text 'agape' meaning a love that is total, unconditional and sacrificial.

The English word of charity is far reaching within the church and is regarded as including generosity, kindness and assistance, all of which fall under the category of giving to those with less than ourselves.

Considered as the decisive accomplishment of the human spirit, the undertaking of giving to another unconditionally is said to reflect God's true nature, and in doing so binds the recipient and beneficiary in divine contact with the Almighty.

It would be the thirteenth century Italian Catholic theologian St. Thomas Aquinas who said of giving; 'Charity, by which God and neighbour are loved, is the most perfect friendship.'

This would give rise to the Catholic Church's thoughts on the acts of generosity as being a primary attainment for all its followers, viewing charity as an outright obligation for humanity's happiness as well as its ultimate objective.

Aquinas' words would accentuate the Bible's teachings, most notably in Paul's First Letter to the Corinthians, Chapter 13.

'When I was a child, I spoke as a child, I understood as a child, I thought as a child, but when I became a man, I put away childish things. For now we see through a glass, darkly; but then face to face, now I know in part; but then shall I know even as also I am known. And now abideth faith, hope, charity, these three; but the greatest of these is charity.'

During the twelfth century, Christianity in the western world expanded its thoughts on charity by way of providing hospitals and medical care for the poor, the funding of which came from rich patrons of the church. It has often been disputed if these 'patrons' gave from pure unconditional philanthropy or if their clemency had ulterior motives, one such being the high regard of an individual gained in society from such noble deeds.

This questioning of the motives behind these actions of generosity links the virtue of charity with its combative sin of avarice. Was it that these patrons gave from the heart with no want of return, or was it purely an act of egotism by the beneficiary so their benevolence would allow them to bask in the esteem of their actions?

As in Buddhism, this questioning of an individual's motives towards giving to others less fortunate than ourselves runs throughout Christian values, yet in searching for the reasons behind such actions it is seen that this advances the follower of Christianity closer to the sanctity of God.

HINDUISM

'Charity given to a worthy person simply because it is right to give, without consideration of anything in return, at the proper place, is stated to be in the mode of goodness.'
The Bhagavad Gita

In ancient Hindu scripture it is stated that 'money alone cannot bring happiness' this is often accompanied by the declaration of 'especially if it is not shared with the poor'.

The act of giving is ingrained within the Hindu religion and although it is seen as acceptable for followers of the faith to pray for money, avarice and its temptations are viewed as intolerable.

Known as 'The Three Gunas' in Hinduism there are three types in which devotees can give to another.

The act of Saattvika is giving as a matter of duty to anyone deserving charity and does nothing in return. This is done specifically at the right place and time.

The second type of generosity is Raajasika which is when something is given unwillingly, or in hope to receive something in return.

The third kind of charity is that of Taamasika when charity is given in the wrong place and time to an unworthy person who pays no respect or holds contempt towards their beneficiary.

The moral and ethical codes of Hinduism all adhere to that of charity and the giving to others freely in the tradition of the aforementioned Saattvika Guna.

With emphasis on the family and their neighbours, devotees of the Hindu faith incorporate the acts of giving in daily life as well as festivals such as Diwali when the giving of others is one of the main themes of the Hindu festival of light.

SIKHISM

'A place in God's court can only be attained if we do service to others in this world.'
Guru Granth Sahib

An integral part of Sikhism is the giving to others freely and with no remorse, this emulates the principle that compassion and equality are important towards the advancement of spiritual life.

This outlook on the generosity of providing charity to others begins within the family home and expands out to the community in which they live, administrating the gifts of money and time towards the building of hospitals, schools and providing care for the less fortunate around them.

A fundamental aspect of Sikhism is the giving of time and energy to helping others within the community. This service to community is called 'Sewa' and is a duty of which followers of Sikhism devote a large portion of their time. Yet, Sewa is not seen as a chore, for it is deemed a privilege for a Sikh to help those around him, be it providing food in the 'Gurdwara' the Sikh place of worship or aiding others of Sikhs in their studies of Sikhism.

CHARITY IN MYTHOLOGY

GREEK

The act of charity and hospitality is known as xenia in Greek mythology.
Translated as 'guest — friend' it is viewed as the deed of bestowing shelter and food towards those travelling far from their own home.

Within this hospitality to travellers the Greek God Zeus is often named Zeus Xenia due to his role of protector towards guests.

In Homer's Iliad, the betrayal of xenia is played out during the battles of the Trojan war, when Paris of the house of Priam of Troy abducts Helen, his host the Spartan King Menelaus' wife.

Seen as an insult to Zeus' sovereignty, it was given to Achilles and his army of Achaeans to avenge the disrespect handed to the God of law and justice.

Regarded as a sequel to the Iliad, Homer's Odyssey portrays the acts of xenia as a running theme throughout his epic poem, when in his ten year journey homewards after the fall of Troy, Odysseus and his soldiers are shown hospitality on their passage from many houses including the house of Circe, to the house of the Phaeacians.

ROMAN

A repeating theme running through Roman mythology concerning the act of charity is the selfless giving of the self to another. This is portrayed in Bernardo Mei's seventeenth century painting 'Roman Charity'.

When Cimon, father of Pero, is sentenced to death by starvation, it is Pero who comes to his aid. In her devotion she sneaks into his prison cell where she then goes on to breastfeed her emaciated father.

This generous action is witnessed by the guards of Cimon's cell and impressed by his daughter's unconditional love Cimon is set free by the authorities.

Pero's story of loyalty to her kin is echoed in Roman mythology when Juno, Queen of the Gods and Goddess of marriage and childbirth, is depicted breastfeeding Hercules.

An Etruscan myth and portrayed in Ruben's 1637 painting 'The Origin of The Milky Way,' whilst Juno slept, her husband Jupiter gave Hercules her breast to feed upon so his son may be bestowed with the Godlike ability of Strength.

On waking, Juno pulled away from the unknown child and the ensuing spraying milk became the Milky Way.

This act of devotion and selflessness would also be portrayed in John Steinbeck's 1939 Pulitzer Prize winning novel 'The Grapes of Wrath.' Set in the economic hardship of the Great Depression, Steinbeck's character, Rose of Sharon, emulates the act of Roman Charity by she herself wet nursing a starving stranger in the corner of a barn.

CHARITY IN ART AND LITERATURE

THE SEVEN WORKS OF MERCY
CARAVAGGIO

Italian painter Caravaggio's 1607 painting 'The Seven Works of Mercy' portrays the seven actions of mercy common to the Catholic faith.

Set as the compassionate deeds carried out towards the welfare of another, Caravaggio painted his work during a stay in Naples for the altarpiece of the Pio Monte della Misericordia Chruch.

The seven mercies pictured are the visiting of prisoners and the feeding of the hungry taken from the myth of Cimon and his daughter Pero, a beggar receiving clothing from St. Martin's cloth, the act of the sheltering of strangers, the burying of the dead, Samson relinquishing his thirst and the visiting of the sick.

Painted to portray the symbolism of charity, The Seven Works of Mercy still hangs in the Pio Monte della Misericordia Church today.

CHARITY AS A MOTHER WITH THREE INFANTS
ANTHONY VAN DYCK

Charity is shown in a different light in Anthony van Dyck's 1627 oil painting of 'Charity' sometimes known under the full title of 'Charity as a Mother with Three Infants.'

Seen as Van Dyck's homage to the contemporary Italian old masters of Titian and Guido Reni, the virtue of charity is viewed as a mother's love in nurturing her children.

This concept was first developed in the fourteenth century before becoming one of the main common allegories to be utilized in art for years to come.

The most important of all the three virtues in the Catholic Church, Charity is often pictured with the other virtues of Faith and Hope.

THE PROPHET
KAHLIL GIBRAN

In Khalil Gibran's' masterpiece on humanity and spiritual advancement, The Prophet talks of giving and explores the view that when you give of yourself then this is the core of true charity. He continues in his subtle teachings to guide others into becoming aware of how those who guard their possessions are only in turn repaid in the fear such actions create.

Our protagonist remains on the subject of charity when speaking of those who own little yet give all are rewarded in their 'coffers' never being empty. This clarifies the theology of world religions in such as it is if those who give with joy then joy shall be their reward.

In advancement of his words, another insight comes forth in the matter of that it may be good to give when asked, but to give wholeheartedly when not prompted is the gesture of which makes God smile on the earth.

Bleak House. A Christmas Carol
Charles Dickens

Dickens' career he would frequently visit the acts of charity and philanthropy, no more so than in his novels of Bleak House and A Christmas Carol.

Published in 1853, Bleak House is classed of one of Dickens' major novels and explores the injustice found within the nineteenth century English legal structure.

As he spent his life concerned with the economic and social differences found throughout Victorian England's class system, Dickens devotes a majority of Bleak House's opening chapter to the ideals of charity and giving in society.

These words were to parallel the history of the times and can lead on to be interpreted as how philanthropy in the upper classes was sometimes viewed as 'providing merit for the soul' in the eyes of the Church.

It would be the 1843 novel A Christmas Carol that would see to being the pinnacle of Dickens' work in defining generosity within humanity's social structure.

The well-known tale tells of Ebenezer Scrooge, the Victorian miser, who is taken on a journey of self-redemption by his deceased business partner Jacob Marley and so is guided towards encountering the apparitions of Christmas past, present and future.

As these specters both terrify and inspire Scrooge's outlook on his penny-pinching ways, Marley's work is completed as his charge comes to recognise the virtues found through the deeds of charity.

THE FOURTH DEADLY SIN

SLOTH

Noun: sloth / 'slôth/
A reluctance to work or make an effort.
"He should overcome his natural sloth and complacency."
Synonyms: laziness, idleness, indolence, slothfulness, inactivity, inertia, sluggishness, apathy, listlessness, lassitude, passivity, lethargy, languor, torpidity.

'We excuse our sloth under the pretext of difficulty.'

Quintilian

An Introduction to Sloth

Taken from the Latin – acedia (without care) and the Greek -aergia (inactivity), Sloth has been portrayed through history in from the mythologies of Roman and Greek origin to the early twentieth century surrealist art movement.

In literature Sloth's penance is shown in the second act of Dante Alighieri's fourteenth century epic poem 'The Divine Comedy' where finding himself in Purgatory, our protagonist Dante and his guide the Roman poet Virgil, encounter the offenders of a lifetime wallowing in sloth. Shakespeare would also utilise the theology behind sloth as a running theme within his work, and can be heard in his comedy 'The Two Gentlemen of Verona' when Valentine tells Proteus:

'I rather would entreat thy company
To see the wonders of the world abroad,
Than living dully sluggardized at home,
Wear out thy youth with shapeless idleness.'
The Two Gentlemen of Verona (1.1.6-9)

Deemed as one of the 'Seven Capital Vices' or 'Cardinal Sins' in the early centuries of Catholicism, this belief is continued to this day and the intricacies of sloth can be found throughout the world's religions.

Commonly perceived as being lazy or apathetic, there are hidden depths within the sin of sloth which are often disguised behind the mask of inactivity. Looked upon in a spiritual sense in the theological philosophies of Buddhism, Christianity and Hinduism, sloth may raise its head in the idleness of others or the self, yet at a deeper level, sloth is construed as an advance towards the avoidance of prayer or duties within the Church or the Temple, and so promotes and causes the eventual distancing from Buddha, God and Shiva.

Due to the complexity surrounding sloth, it can be a difficult transgression to perceive in others. When an individual's appearance portrays a peaceful mind, what could be interpreted as serenity may in fact be sloth's subtleties. The delicate creeping of sloth's manipulation can leave its quarry unaware of the depths to which the sin has embedded within them. Lost in sloth's embrace no effort is needed to either confront or surmount to life's challenges. This ultimately accentuates the avoidance of said victim's spiritual path.

SLOTH IN RELIGION

BUDDHISM

'This Dharma is for developing energy, not for developing laziness.'
Gautama Buddha

The sin of sloth is recognised in Buddhism as one of the 'Five Hindrances,' a list of burdens said to hinder the act of daily meditation within Buddhist devotees.

Seen as obstacles towards attaining a high medative state, sloth and its associate torpor, a state of physical or mental inactivity promoting lethargy in an individual, are joined by the hindrances of sensory desire, ill will, restlessness, and doubt.

In the Buddhist branch of the Mahayana tradition, these interferences are seen to obstruct a practitioner in reaching 'Samatha', the calming of the mind through the mindfulness of breathing to reach a tranquil state in meditation.

Sloth as part of the Five Hindrances can be further defined in four symptomatic states of mind ranging from boredom to a withdrawal from life's difficulties and hardships.

When the familiar around an individual holds no delight and what was once stimulating to the senses becomes the ordinary, it is then that boredom enters sloth's arena. From this state of mind arises the temptation of pursuing new levels of stimulation in our surrounding environment and so mislaying our knowledge that a developed awareness affords the happiness our soul craves in the realisation of completion.

Complacency in meditation is an indirect manifestation of sloth and torpor. This occurs in the most subtle of ways, for when the meditation process is not only succeeding but also attained time and time again, so complacency of the situation creeps in. This often leaves the meditator to mislay that longed for element of effervescence and vitality in their practice. It is then that sloth gains entrance into the mind of the practitioner.

Closely linked to complacency is the action of the mind sinking into the tranquillity of Samatha. This happens when the serenity reached for in meditation is achieved and the practitioner falls into the comfort and wellbeing of this state. This can cause an imbalance and override the alertness of mind needed within the practice of meditation, giving sloth an opportunity to devour a meditator's dream like thoughts.

When facing any inner difficulties which may arise within our lives from time to time it can be easy to withdraw from such moments. This pulling back can interfere with the process of meditation. In the retreat from worry, the meditator lacks the strength necessary to deal with the problem at hand. Unable to connect with the vitality needed to confront their difficulties a distraction is often found in sloth and torpor where the meditator can take shelter in the false security the sin offers, and so finding comfort in the notion that in by withdrawing from the situation no effort is needed to meet with the challenges before us.

Buddhists believe that in becoming aware of these Five Hindrances sloth can be tackled within our daily lives and through the act of meditation and the mindfulness of being, sloth can often be held at bay, as can its accomplice torpor.

CHRISTIANITY

'How long will you lie down, O sluggard? When will you arise from your sleep? "A little sleep, a little slumber. A little folding of the hands to rest." - Your poverty will come in like a vagabond. And your need like an armed man.'
Proverbs 6: 9

Sloth in Christianity is thought of as a complex and intricate transgression in that the subtlety of the sin can be disguised in the emotions of serenity and calmness in an individual.

This tranquil state can mask sloth in giving said individual the appearance of living in peace. Yet this is viewed within the Church as being sloth's ploy for humankind, to bask in the comfort of not having to make an effort in taking priority to do what is needed for the advancement along our own unique spiritual path.

A form of 'spiritual sloth' is recognised in Catholicism in numerous degrees concerning working life, these include the indolence of some who work with the essence of reluctance, those who procrastinate about doing anything worthwhile, and those who refuse to work at all.

Relative to the ethics behind these slothful avoidances of work, it is remembered that God placed Adam and Eve in the Garden of Eden in avoidance of these reasons.

'So, the Lord God took the man (He had made) and settled him in the Garden of Eden to cultivate and keep it.'
Genesis 2: 15

Another practice of sloth is associated with spiritual exercises and duties, where a dislike for prayer or devotion leads the believer to step back from God and His words therein.

Understood as wasting valuable time, Christianity look sternly on those who give themselves to sloth in evading a lifetime of the demands a spiritual journey makes.

Known as one of the 'Seven Capital Vices' or 'Cardinal Sins' in the Roman Catholic Church, sloth also went under the title of 'acedia' a Latin word taken from the Greek script for 'negligence.'

Each sin within the Roman Catholic Church was invariably placed in to two different kinds of sin; a venial sin which is forgiven through reparation and a mortal sin that merits damnation with no reconciliation. Depending on the particulars of the sin committed, the seven deadly sins may be counted as venial or mortal.

As in the case of sloth it is usually seen as a venial sin when an individual shows only a slight effect of laziness and apathy about them, and so does not breach their relationship with God.

If, however, sloth is deeply embedded within the sinner and a refusal to work escalates to a point where their family cannot be fed, clothed or housed, then this is deemed as falling into the category of being a mortal sin, the damnation of which for sloth is the punishment of being thrown into a writhing pit of snakes in depths of hell.

HINDUISM

'Sad is the steadfastness wherewith the fool cleaves to his sloth, his sorrow, and his fears, his folly and despair.
This - Pritha's Son! – Is born of Tamas, "dark" and miserable.'
The Bhagavad Gita

A philosophical concept developed by the Samkhya school of Hindu philosophy, sloth is accredited with the Sanskrit title of Tamas, or darkness.

Alongside the two qualities of Sattva which holds the values of goodness, purity and harmony, and Rajas, passion, drive and self-motivation, Tamas is viewed as having the non-desirable attributes of apathy, inertia and inactivity.

In Indian philosophy, Sattva, Raja and Tamas are looked upon as being present within everyone. With no-one solely having one of these three characteristics, all three are seen to play in complex interaction within the human psyche in varying degrees of intensity.

Hindu attitudes urge followers of Hinduism to put great effort into their lives and to recognise when Tamas is at play in their emotions, the troubles of which can lead the sufferer to acts of the deferment of spiritual matters and general laziness and lethargy.

These thoughts are defined in the Tamil poet and philosopher, Tiru Valluvar, who in his great ethical work of 'Kural' also known as the 'Thirukkural' says of sloth:

'Procrastination, forgetfulness, laziness and sleep--these four form the coveted ship which bears men to their destined ruin; Seldom do men possessed by sloth achieve anything special, even when supported by the earth's wealthy proprietors; The lazy ones, inept in noble exertion, invite sharp scoldings and must endure the shame of scornful words.'
Thirukkural

SLOTH IN MYTHOLOGY

GREEK

It seems only fitting that Aergia, the Goddess of Sloth and Laziness should guard the Underworld court of Hypnos the God of Sleep.

Daughters of Aether, God of the Air in which the Gods breath, and Gaia, Goddess of the Earth and mother to the one eyed giant Cyclopes, Aergia sits outside the opening of Hypnos' cave home beside her fellow sentinels Quies, Oblivio and Otia, the Gods of Quiet, Forgetfulness and Ease.

Although Dionysus God of wine is more suited to the sin of gluttony, he can also be classed as a participant of sloth.

This fraction of his persona is found in the consumption of alcohol, where throughout history the taking of alcohol has been viewed as an escape from life's pressures and anxieties, and so provides its partaker respite from the challenges supposed to be met both as in the eyes of faith, spiritually, and within the physical world around us.

This avoidance can be read as a gateway towards sloth's embrace, where the essence of following a spiritual path and the want of ambition and zeal in an individual's material development matters little behind a veil of drunken haze.

ROMAN

Murcia, a Deity of Sloth and Idleness, is known for her proficiency of inactivity and is also named Myrtus through her connection to the symbolism of Venus, the Goddess of Love.

Murcia is said to have lived in a temple in the shadows of the Aventine Hill, one of the seven hills on which ancient Rome was built, and for visitors who happened to enter her temple Murcia's slothfulness would soon overpower her unwitting guests.

SLOTH IN ART AND LITERATURE

THE SLOTHFUL
SALVADOR DALI

Inspired by Dante's Divine Comedy, between the years of 1951 and 1960 the Catalonian surrealist painter Salvador Dali created 101 water colour drawings on wooden blocks depicting Dante's journey through Hell, Purgatory and the Paradise of Heaven.

In Dali's interpretation of sloth, on a plain background Dante and Virgil are seen standing before a halo adorned kneeling figure in the act of prayer. As Dante's arms transform and melt into the a swirling red cloth representing the running crowds destined to rush around Purgatory's fourth tier, Virgil can be seen behind Dante, pulling him back from sloth's clutches.

INDOLENCE (LA PARESSEUSE ITALIENNE)
JEAN-BAPTISTE GREUZE

Painted in 1757 by the French master Jean-Baptiste Greuze, Indolence would be one of four paintings of the 'dans le costume Italien' series that depicted life within Italy.

Influenced by the work of Italian artist Caravaggio's Baroque style, Indolence (La Paresseuse Italienne), translated to English as the lazy Italian, portrays the lethargy of spirit which sloth can induce within the soul.

The woman pictured in his work sits slouched in a chair surrounded by plates and pans discarded on the floor around her. Her apathetic expression matches her current outlook on life as she is shown to have given up half way through putting her shoes on, with the final shoe seen cast on the floor on its side in the forefront of the painting.

THE DIVINE COMEDY: PURGATORY
DANTE ALIGHIERI

Purgatory, the second part of Dante Alighieri's early fourteenth century epic poem 'The Divine Comedy' offers insight into the sin of sloth.

As Dante stands beside his guide the Roman poet Virgil on Purgatory's fourth tier, both are distracted by the rush of a crowd streaming past them, each member of the throng calling out tales of haste from history.

One figure pauses to talk with Dante and Virgil. Telling them he was once the abbot of Verona's St. Zeno, his words fade from the two as he is caught up and carried away in the continues melee of hurrying crowds.

It is then that Virgil explains to Dante that what they are witnessing are those who have spent their lifetimes held within sloths grasp, and so now their penance is to constantly run around Purgatory's fourth tier.

WILLIAM SHAKESPEARE

Shakespeare would include the principles of sloth in many of his works. From the historic to the tragic and to the comic, sloth would become a running theme.

From the historical plays of Henry VI and Henry VIII to the tragedy of Cymbeline and in his tragi-comedy The Tempest, the subtlety of the sin's composition is shown in the words of Shakespeare's characters.

Awake, awake, English nobility!
Let not sloth dim your horrors new-begot.
Henry VI (1.1.79-80), Messenger

And to the English court assemble now,
From every region, apes of idleness!
Henry VI (4.5.125-6), Henry IV

These cardinals trifle with me; I abhor
This dilatory sloth and tricks of Rome.

Henry VIII (2.4.255-6), King Henry

Hereditary sloth instructs me.
The Tempest (2.1.241), Sebastian

Weariness
Can snore upon the flint, when resty sloth
Finds the down pillow hard.
Cymbeline (3.6.35-7), Belarius

THE FOURTH HEAVENLY VIRTUE

DILIGENCE

Noun: diligence / ˈdĭl'ə-jəns/
Careful and persistent work or effort.
"His diligence was of great tenacity."
Synonyms: conscientiousness, assiduousness,
assiduity, industriousness, rigour, rigorousness,
punctiliousness, sedulousness, heedfulness, earnestness.

'To be idle is a short road to death and to be diligent is a way of life; foolish people are idle, wise people are diligent.'

Gautama Buddha

An Introduction to Diligence

Of all the Heavenly virtues, Diligence is regarded as being the most noblest.

From Buddhism to Christianity and those following Hindu beliefs, diligence of mind is seen as essential in the advancement of a believer's spiritual path, in this life time to some and in all lifetimes to come to others.

Presented as persistence of spirit, the importance of diligence in an individual is viewed in differing reasons in cultures around the world.

Buddhists see the virtue as being of upmost importance in the practice of meditation, where in cultivating diligence leads to the avoidance of any distraction caused by diligence's opposing force, the deadly sin of sloth.

Christianity, or more notably the Roman Catholic Church, has the view that on having diligence of character an individual shows the traits of dependability and a zeal for life. These qualities are needed for entrance into Heaven and all continued within.

The characteristics of persistence and effort are also well documented within Greek mythology by Homer, throughout his epic tale of the Odyssey, where Odysseus persisted through great hardships on his immense journey of courage and self-discovery.

In all the theological and mythological scripts on diligence, it is within the individual to partake in having this virtue accompany them on their life path.

No matter if said individual is under the watchful gaze of Buddha, God or Shiva, it is of such importance to allow persistence of mind into our lives, for without these qualities a lifetime is spent filled with sedentary moments where any ambition and drive is put aside, often due to the daunting effort needed in which to achieve such dreams.

When the veil to diligence has been lifted there is another extra factor of the diligent virtue, in that there becomes a need for extra persistence of mind, a requirement to cultivate and tend to the most precious of virtues.

DILIGENCE IN RELIGION

BUDDHISM

'Chaos is inherent in all compounded things. Strive on with diligence...'
The last words of Buddha

Diligence in Buddhism is regarded as one of the most important values in Buddha's teachings, as without diligence the practice of meditation that plays such a central role within the followers of the Buddha cannot be advanced.

It is seen that through diligence and perseverance of spirit that only then can an individual achieve the attainment of enlightenment, and as Buddha said in his teachings 'the lazy person is far from enlightenment.'

By practicing diligence either in daily meditation or the pursuit of spiritual advancement, Buddhists believe that life around us becomes to be perceived as having greater importance and meaning, where the knowledge of the individual increases dramatically and the distracting corruption of laziness and apathy are seen for the interferences they truly are, thus dispelling all suffering from the soul and transcending the perception of humanity within its place in the world.

Often going under the title of 'enthusiastic perseverance', diligence of spirit can also be observed as having the element of curiosity within an individual which ultimately leads to an enthusiastic desire to learn. This in turn leads to shunning the disruptions of any idleness or languid thoughts our mind may harbour.

Alongside generosity, morality, tolerance, meditation and wisdom, diligence is the fourth of the 'Six Perfections' in Buddhist teachings that tells of the six traits of the human character which need perfecting before the arrival of enlightenment.

In the Tibetan Mahayana tradition of Buddhism, the virtue of diligence is the third 'Paramiti' - Sanskit for perfection or completeness, which are then divided into three factions, these being Parami, Upa Parami, and Paramattha Parami.

Seen as the demeanour in which we conduct our lives and our view on the parameters of the world, Paramita is at times considered as meaning the deeds of transcendental actions, where the ego is enthused to shed its vain and conceited behaviours.

In the Theravada (old school) Buddhist tradition of South East Asia, diligence along with effort, vigour and energy, are observed as being 'Virya Paramita', defined as an unreserved want to engage in wholesome activities as to accomplish results from virtuous actions.

Promoting persistence and diligence within the individual, Virya is regarded as the continuous and unrelenting effort in overpowering the vices of ill will and the deceitful actions towards others and the indulging in immoral activities such as gambling sensual desire. These vices are all viewed as an unhealthy influence on the practitioner of meditation and can only be eliminated in the sustained effort of the cultivation of diligence.

With this view of utilizing the persistence of spirit in the individual towards the avoidance of lethargy and languor, through refining conscientiousness and compassion within an individual's core spiritual foundations it is recognised in all branches of Buddhism, be it in the Tibetan Mahayana tradition or in Theravada beliefs, that by practicing and achieving diligence in life there is nothing which cannot be achieved.

CHRISTIANITY

'Blessed is the man who remains steadfast under trial, for where he has stood the test he will receive the crown of life, which God has promised to those who love Him.'
Proverbs 6: 6-8

In the matters of faith, diligence in the eyes of the Christian Church is the completeness of the persistent actions of a parishioner to reach a state of spiritual success in their lives.

The importance of keeping diligent whilst confronted with life's challenges and trials and still retaining faith in God can be found throughout the Bible.

In the Christian Church, some of the characteristic traits of diligence are identified as being self-motivated, punctual and in having the ability to persevere without complaining.

These qualities are regarded as being found in the actions of adhering to God's calling. In being dependable and striving to meet goals, it is observed that a Christian retaining the virtue of diligence also holds a similar tenacity towards prayer.

Noted as one of the Capital Virtues in the Catholic Church and the corrective solution towards the sin of sloth, diligence is observed as an instruction to fulfil duties within life, even when chores and responsibilities are either too painful to confront or too laborious to partake in.

These duties in life can include work, home life and families, as well as an individual's faith and belief in God.

The Catholic Church sees prayer as an answer to those who are not adept at utilising diligence in their life. Instilling the practice of prayer in those who shy away from life's tribulations by avoiding the persistence needed within situations of conflict, the Church's application of verse and canto are considered a remedy to such lethargy, be it in the work environment or arising in problems between spouses. This is confirmed in the words of Timothy of Lystra, Asia Minor.

'Take pains with these things; be absorbed in them, so that your progress will be evident to all. Pay close attention to yourself and to your teaching; persevere in these things, for as you do this you will ensure salvation both for yourself and for those who hear you.'
2 Timothy 4: 15-16

Although viewed that to embrace diligence is take a step closer to God, it is essential how an individual enacts the diligence needed in these steps closer to the Almighty.

To take to a task at hand through necessity and not surrender to diligence's virtues, then this is touching on the outer edges of sloth, for it said that the way a believer accomplishes their tasks on earth will in turn define Christ's judgement on how they shall spend the rest of eternity.

HINDUISM

'Who so performeth diligent, content, the work allotted him, whatever it be, lays hold of perfectness.'
The Bhagavad-Gita

In Hinduism, the Dharma, the path of righteousness and conduct, is to live through correct intention, the concern for the wellbeing of others and with diligence of spirit.

The theology behind these thoughts within the Dharma lead a Hindu worshiper to discover the qualities of diligence, and so are then able to employ this virtue in daily life.

The Hindu Goddess Lakshmi symbolises diligence and honesty and she is a focus of worship during the Hindu celebrations of Diwali.

Known as the festival of light, Diwali is celebrated yearly during the months of October or November by the Gregorian calendar and under the Hindu Lunisolar calendar during the new moon of the month of Kartika.

With India's Hindu devotees celebrating the victory of light over darkness, Nepal's Hindu community also celebrate Diwlai under the title of Tihar.

For three days and nights Kathmandu's streets are lit by candle light, with candles leading from the street and through the doorways of shops and homes to encourage good luck for the coming year. For as well as being the Goddess of Diligence, Lakshmi is also known as the Goddess of Wealth and Prosperity.

It is in Lakshmi's duel concepts that diligence takes an important place within her attributes, in that to achieve wealth the Hindu followers must show persistence of thought as to achieve their desired riches, yet with not forgetting to show the Dharma's teachings of concern for others during their pursuit for prosperity.

DILIGENCE IN MYTHOLOGY

GREEK

The son of Gaia the Earth Goddess and Uranus God of the Sky, Hyperion the God of Heavenly Light was recorded as the first to recognise the seasons of the world and the movement of the sun, moon and stars. The result of Hyperion's persistence and want of understanding in all around him leading to these observations attributed to him, it would be because of his insight into the workings of world and sky that he would come to be known as the 'father of heavenly bodies'.

The theme of diligence in Greek mythology also includes that of Theseus.

Son of Aethra and by the two fathers of Aegeus and God of the Sea, Earthquakes and Horses, Theseus would become the King of Athens due to his heroic nature and persistent want for justice within his land. These traits would be written about in various forms, most notably through the myth of Theseus' confrontation with the half man half bull creature the Minotaur.

On the island of Crete in the underground labyrinth constructed by Deadalus who also made wings for his son Icarus, the Minotaur sat within its center devouring those who wandered onto his path.

Volunteering to put an end to the Minotaur's ways, Theseus sailed to Crete where he then fell in love with King Minos' daughter, Ariadne, Goddess of Mazes, Paths, Fertility and Passion.

On Deadalus' recommendation, Ariadne gave Theseus a ball of thread so he may find his way back to the labyrinth's entrance.

Entering the labyrinth Theseus did as instructed and tied one end of the thread to the entrance and made his way through the myriad of passageways leading to the Minotaur's domain.

On reaching the middle of the labyrinth he found the Minotaur he had come to slay sleeping, only to awaken on Theseus' approach. A mammoth fight ensued, the results of which ended in Theseus beheading the creature and retracing his steps with the aid of the Ariadne's thread until he appeared from the labyrinth, the Minotaur's head held high above him.

ROMAN

Although closely linked with the myths of diligence seen in Greek mythology, there are several Roman minor Gods and Goddesses whose persistence and diligence of spirit fuelled myths of heroic acts involving the tenacity of heart.

Victoria was seen as the Goddess of Victory and was often prayed to by Roman soldiers wanting protection on the eve of battle within her determined conducts of winning against all odds.

The Goddess of Justive, Justita, would also be called upon in Roman times, for it was she who emitted the diligence of truth to appear before those who cast doubt on another's actions.

Of all these minor Gods it would be Hercules, the God of Strength, whose diligence surpassed that of mere mortals, seen in his persistence of righteousness for others played out in the courageous deeds recorded throughout ancient Roman literature.

DILIGENCE IN ART AND LITERATURE

THE SISTINE CHAPEL
MICHAEL ANGELO

Reflecting probably one of the greatest examples of diligence in the world of art history is Michael Angelo's ceiling of the Vatican City's the Sistine Chapel.

Painted between the years of 1508 and 1512, Michael Angelo was relentlessly hounded by the then Pope Julius II to finish the masterpiece, spending up to twelve hours at a time laying on his back on a wooden platform high above the chapel's polished marble flooring creating his depictions of Biblical scenes.

From the story of Noah to the centrepiece of the 'Creation of Adam', Michael Angelo's diligence and persistence of thought in not giving up even when under extreme physical discomfort and immense pressure from the Catholic Church shone through in the sheer beauty and completion of the magnificent ceiling of the Sistine Chapel.

THE PERSISTENCE OF MEMORY
SALVADOR DALI

Salvador Dali's 1931 painting is regarded as having an array of meanings and hidden subtleties towards the emotions experienced when within the surrealist dreamtime state.

Elements within the work can be inferred as contributing to the theology behind the Heavenly virtue of Diligence, in that the melting clocks in the centre of the piece are amongst other ideas, a metaphorical example of the softness at times present in the human spirit.

This one of many theories is coupled with what is said to be Dali's own profile laying in a sleeping position on the wide open beachscape and the display of ants in the foreground of the painting signifying the decay of mind.

Diligence can therefore be viewed as a gateway out of the apathy displayed in the clearing of clouds in the background and the evidence of an emerging dawn.

TO KILL A MOCKING BIRD
HARPER LEE

In Harper Lee's Pulitzer Prize winning novel 'To Kill a Mocking Bird' the virtue of diligence is at the heart of the book.

Published in 1960, it tells the story of lawyer Atticus Finch, who in the depression era of America's deep southern states defends the rights of the wrongly accused.

Finch's want for justice is identified as the persistence of mind in that amid the racial tensions of the times and under the doubt of others, he casts such prejudices aside in his quest for the truth and in doing so provides an insight into the attributes of such a virtue to his children.

THE OLD MAN AND THE SEA
ERNEST HEMMINGWAY

Pulitzer Prize winning American novel, The Old Man of the Sea also explores the Heavenly virtue of Diligence.

Published in 1952, and the last of Hemmingway's major fictional works, his book would also convey the heart of persistence of spirit in humanity.

The story of an elderly Cuban fisherman who is edging towards sloth's realm and decides to head out to sea to break his eighty day plus dry spell of not achieving a notable catch. Tormented by his village's younger fishermen, the old man sets to sea in hope of catching a prized marlin.

Sailing out in his small boat away from the shores of his home he soon happens upon hooking a marlin the likes of which he has never witnessed before. Yet the old man's boat is dragged out to sea by the gigantic fish.

Through acute diligence he manages to tire the beast and eventually ties the marlin to the side of his boat and makes homewards to parade his triumphant catch.

It is in his return to land that the diligence once so strong within the old man's younger days is tested when a group of sharks discover his quarry.

The Fifth Deadly Sin

WRATH

Noun: wrath / ˈrɒθ/
Anger taken to the extreme.
"Her wrath knew no bounds."
Synonyms: anger, rage, fury, annoyance, indignation, outrage,
hot temper, bad mood, ill humour, spleen, irritability,
cantankerousness, querulousness, crabbiness, testiness.

'Come not between the dragon and his wrath.'

King Lear (I, i, 124)
William Shakespeare

An Introduction to Wrath

The fifth deadly sin of wrath is the culmination of anger that escalates into rage or blind fury within a person.

Often portrayed in its physical form, Wrath can also manifest itself in an individual by the act of spurning love from others and internalising anger to a point where this is all that resides within the heart.

Self-righteousness is another aspect of wrath where the soul's denial of truth within itself and others often leads to inappropriate feelings of anger directed at both parties. The root of a want for revenge for the injustice presented by another, it would be Dante Alighieri the fourteenth century Italian scribe who said of wrath, "love of justice perverted to revenge and spite".

The internalisation of wrath is observed in the Catholic Church as being self-centred anger brought about by an impatience towards another's actions which is coupled by a want to punish them.

In Buddhist traditions the sin of wrath is noted as one of the Five Hindrances that inhibits the cultivation of meditation practices within an individual. This internal conflict in a believer's souls can also be found in the Three Poisons. Alongside the poison's two contemporaries of ignorance and greed, wrath obstructs the progression of spiritual paths both of a devotee and those surrounding them that fall foul of another's fury.

Acknowledged in religions across the world, wrath's traits are portrayed in parables and verse as uncontrolled anger and a desire to seek retribution. Within scriptures this want of revenge is seen as never being sated after the act of revenge has been performed and so leaving an individual consumed by the sin of wrath to continue in its furious grasp.

WRATH IN RELIGION

CHRISTIANITY

'Refrain from anger, and forsake wrath! Fret not yourself; it tends only to evil.'
Psalms 37: 8

There are several aspects in which the deadly sin of wrath can be referenced to in the Christian Church. Viewed as an aspect of both God and man, it is God's wrath that is more popularly known.

Regarded as a 'Divine Wrath', the wrath of God is justified in that He holds a complete absence of malice or indignation towards all sentinel beings. Through this absolute divinity, God's wrath is shown in the metaphorical sense through acts of natural ruin against those who apply deliberate will towards the carrying out of particular sins. Yet, with God's wrath focused upon those committing such inexcusable deeds there remains compassion deep within His actions, where forgiveness with understanding is administrated with the knowledge of 'they know not what they do'.

'Human Wrath' is seen within the Church as humankind engaging in extreme anger that reaches the height of fury, and so resulting in wrath and a failing in those believers who let its emotional disturbance enter their spirit through weakness of faith.

In the eyes of the Catholic Church wrath is seen as a sin every individual at one time or another can fall victim to and is viewed as a self-centred anger generated by impatience towards others and a desire to punish them.

Anger within a believer is said to take many forms from a hot temper to having an aggressive nature be it physical or passive.

Recognised as contributing characteristic that causes the breakdown of marriages, friendships and other emotional relationships, wrath is not only demonstrated in physical forms but also internally. This occurs when an individual turns his anger away from the world and harbours animosity within his heart.

Seen as an unholy alliance with two of the other deadly sins of pride and envy, when wrath is joined by these transgressions repressed anger can lead to an unprecedented breakdown of faith and the hope thereof which lays within.

At the core of this internal anger a lack of power becomes a driving force for wrathful emotions. This can be observed in modern day times as anxiety towards losing a job, a relationship or wealth and material possessions, where fear and self-doubt in an individual's own abilities pushes to the fore.

A result of these insecurities concealed within, a soul manifests a brusk and defensive manner, pushing away those who may at times only be trying to help those they see in such pain and torment from spending so long holding such anger within them.

In seeing a member of their congregation sheltering wrath's traits, the Church guides the follower to the heavenly virtue of patience to counteract rage's attempted demise of the soul's true spirit.

HINDUISM

'The man of wrath who, surrounded by darkness, always inflicts, by help of his own energy, various kinds of punishment on persons whether they deserve them or not, is necessarily separated from his friends in consequence of that energy of his.'
The Mahabharata

Within Hinduism it is believed that an individual suffering from the effects of wrath cannot carry out their life paths when instilled with the emotional content of rage and anger.

Viewed as receiving sorrow and unhappiness formed from a want for unfulfilled desires of life's pleasures, wrath can be considered as the culmination of frustration within an individual.

As an indication of ignorance resulting in an unending oppression within the believer, wrath and its ideologies are featured in the Bhagavad Gita as being a total engagement with attachment to money, material goods or at times, people.

Wrath is also defined in the result of having and retaining frustration in an individual's life. This can be observed in an incessant want for wealth and material items, of which those suffering from the sin of wrath reason that this will satisfy the anger harboured inside their soul.

Throughout Hindu theology in both scripture and oral history, the Gods of Hinduism are considered quick to temper and to have a fiery disposition.

One of the Hindu Gods who is believed to have a hot temperament is that of the Goddess Kali.

Considered as being the Goddess of death, Kali is widely worshiped in Hinduism where her image is represented as wearing a garland of skulls around her neck. Through her alarming depiction, the followers of Hindu values pay their respects to Kali and her companion Lord Shiva, in fear of any retribution that may be administrated to them from the Gods.

BUDDHISM

'He who can curb his wrath as soon as it arises, as a timely antidote will check snake's venom that so quickly spreads - such a monk gives up the here and the beyond, just as a serpent sheds its worn-out skin.'
Gautama Buddha

Rage, fury and anger all fall into the categories of the deadly sin of wrath as seen in Buddhism.

Regarded as aversion and translated as zhe sdang in Tibetan Buddhist tradition, wrath is presented as one of the Kleshas which are seen as emotional states that bring confusion to the soul resulting in an individual to perform acts of objectionable activities.

Of the three root Kleshas of Moha - aberration and confusion, Raga - attachment and avarice, ill will and wrath towards another is represented by Dvesha, the third of these three sicknesses within an individual's character which leads them to continue the circle of re-birth and so be susceptible to suffering.

Represented by a snake within the hub of The Wheel of Life, Bhavachakra, Dvesha also embodies the poison of ignorance within an individual, noted to be as self destructive as wrath.

Indicated as the three poisons in the Tibetan Mahayana tradition of Buddhism and as the three unwholesome roots in South East Asia's Theravada tradition, as with Dvesha's counterparts of Moha and Raga, these afflictions of mind are considered an ultimate distraction towards the application and cultivation of meditative practices.

The appearance of ill will within a devotee can be directed not only at another but also inwardly where a supreme distaste for meditation enters and individual's essence. This directs attention onto other distractions and at times can lead to transferring a dislike towards all surrounding an individual. This in turn can lead to the aversion of their own soul and so force attention to wander beyond the self.

As an extension of the Three Poisons, wrath and its traits also feature within Buddhism's Five Hindrances.

Alongside lust, sloth, the doubt in the self and in others, and the incompetence for the mind to receive stillness, the ill will of an individual is viewed as becoming focused on emotions rooted in umbrage, vengeance and antagonistic actions, as well as wrath.

The antidote for any of these hindrances is found in processing what the mind displays to a devotee when either in a medative state or not. By first identifying and more importantly recognising a problem of ill will has arisen within the devotees mind, the next step is to accept such thoughts no matter how destructive they may be.

Once these two steps have been accomplished it is then necessary to show curiosity towards the affliction and question what may be the motives behind such emotions and how they are affecting the mind in which they have settled.

When the analysis of the hindrance is complete it is then of necessity to further the meditation practice. This is done by concentrating on deeds of love and kindness, resulting in an understanding that these hurtful emotions of the mind are merely a passing process which will come and go throughout our lives until our impulses are mastered. These realisations bring the foresight that both the three poisons and the Five Hindrances are not who we are.

WRATH IN MYTHOLOGY

GREEK

The Manae (mania) were an assembly of personified spirits representing Madness, Anger and Wrath. The children of the primordial Nyx, their innate joy of revenge and torment, the Manae would be closely linked to the Erinyes.

The three Goddesses of Vengeance, Retribution and Penance, the Erinyes, would utilise their Wrath in punishing mortals who had committed crimes against the Gods. Their methods would include inducing insanity and fits of rage onto those who had made such acts.

Carrying whips, the Erinyes were portrayed as winged women who also served Hades in his Underworld Kingdom, inflicting torturous chastisements upon those residing within. With the Manae and the Erinyes prompting wrath into the souls of both men and Gods, it would be their sister Lyssa who would be truly identified with the deadly sin of wrath. Daughter of Nyx, the primordial Goddess of the Night who was formed at the beginning of Earth's creation, and fathered by the spilt blood of Ouranus (Uranus) the primordial God of the Sky, Lyssa's attributes of anger included that of being able to coax another into uncontrollable rage, be they mortal or immortal beings.

Lyssa's abilities in encouraging wrath in others was shown when the Goddess of Marriage and Childbirth, Hera, called upon Lyssa's abilities.

Hera's distain for the God of Strength came from not only her envy of Hercules' might and hero status amongst the people of ancient Greece and those of Mount Olympus of which he was the gatekeeper, but also for the adulterous actions of her husband Zeus, King of the Gods and father of Hercules. With this great animosity, Hera summoned Lyssa to instil Hercules with wrath. Much to Lyssa's protests she soon submitted to Hera's wishes and one night drove Hercules to such a blind rage that he killed his wife Megara and their children. Another facet attributed to the personified spirit of rage was Lyssa's patronage of rabies. This was shown in the myth of the Greek hero Actaen and Artemis the Goddess of Chastity and the Hunt.

When Artemis discovered Actaen bathing naked in a lake one hot summer's day her wrath at his disrespect for the Gods prompted her to change the fateful bather into a stag. Arriving at the scene, Lyssa inflicted rabies onto each of the dogs belonging to Actaen, which then proceeded to rip the hero's body apart.

ROMAN

Although wrath is more attributed to mythology in ancient Greece, wrath's counterparts are significant in Roman literature. The personification of Anger, Lyssa, had her Roman equivalent in that of Ira and Furor, as did the Manea (mania) who in Greek mythology were the spirits of Madness and Insanity, and in Roman mythology the spirits of Death and the mothers of ghosts who enrage the living.

WRATH IN ART AND LITERATURE

GUERNICA
PABLO PICASSO

Wrath is displayed throughout Picasso's 1937 painting Guernica.

Using only a palette of grey, white and black, the three feet high by nearly eight foot wide mural on canvas shows the artist's contempt and rage towards the bombing of the Spanish Basque town of the paintings title during the Spanish Civil War.

Targeted for being a believed stronghold of the Republican resistance made up of Communists, Socialists and Anarchists, the bombing was initiated on the request of the Spanish National government by both the German and Fascist Italian air force.

Reports of mortal casualties differ with estimates of between one hundred and one and a half thousand, the resulting confusion due to the Spanish Nationalists playing down the true number of victims of the atrocity.

So incensed by the destruction of innocent lives, Picasso started painting Guernica within a week of the bombing of his homeland.

Becoming one of his most celebrated works, Picasso's decision to use only black, white and grey came from the want of portraying the massacre in the photographic newsworthy style of the times, most notably as seen in the Hungarian photographer Robert Capa's own photographic documentation of the Spanish Civil War one year earlier.

Picasso's wrath to the injustice and bloodshed shown on the streets of Guernica are seen in his use of a bull and a horse in the composition, with both animals not only representing Spain but also the strength and courage within the Spanish people. These values can be surmised as Picasso's defiance towards the Fascist movement and its building spread across Europe in the late 1930's.

PROMETHEUS BOUND
PAUL RUBENS

The seventeenth century Flemish artist Peter Paul Rubens spent most of his career focusing on producing large paintings of scenes with a theological theme. However, in 1612 he began 'Prometheus Bound' a painting inspired by Zeus's punishment to Prometheus found in works of ancient Greek literature.

Using a Baroque style, Prometheus Bound depicts Zeus' wrath towards the Titan, where chained to a rock beneath a tree Prometheus lays naked in torment. His anguished expression is brought about by the large eagle above him with wings spread wide gorging on Prometheus' liver. This punishment administered by Zeus resulted from the Titan's love for all mankind.

When Prometheus and his brother Epimetheus were given the task of creating man, it would be Prometheus who shaped man's form out of clay, bringing him to life with aid of Athena the Goddess of wisdom and courage who then gave man the breathe of life.

As his brother was making man, Epimetheus had the duty of giving animals various qualities of flight, cunning and stealth. When it came for him to bestow such qualities onto man, in his foolishness he had exhausted his supply and nothing left to give. It was then that Prometheus gave man the ability to stand up and walk and presented his creation with the gift of fire. When Prometheus tricked Zeus into thinking a sacrificial offering had come from man, Zeus' rage saw him take fire away from man to punish Prometheus in the knowledge of his great love for humankind.

On hearing of Zeus' actions Prometheus lit a torch on the Sun and gave fire back to man. This caused such burning wrath within the King of the Gods that he chained Prometheus to a rock and instructed an eagle to eat the Titan's liver, only for the liver to regenerate overnight ready for the eagle's feast the next day, and the next day, and the next.

A CLOCKWORK ORANGE
ANTHONY BURGESS

Narrated by Alex, a fifteen year old boy living in a dystopian future of inner city London, Anthony Burgess' novel A Clockwork Orange would portray wrath through the acts of mindless viciousness combined with rage towards others for no other reason than wanting to partake in 'a little of the old ultraviolence'.

Using the language of Nadsat, a slang created by the author using a mixture of Russian and olde English throughout the book, Alex's story unfolds in him being the leader of the Droogs, a group of young men who show their dissatisfaction with life and disregard for another's soul in unprovoked violent actions towards those they take a fancy to.

When Alex is caught by the authorities after carrying out the brutal murder of the wife of the author F. Alexander, he is sentenced to fourteen years in prison. After two years of incarceration, F. Alexander happens upon Alex and offers him an end to his imprisonment if he partakes in an experiment designed to rid wrath from an individual through the heartless procedure of the Ludovico technique. Agreeing to be the first to try the technique, Alex is subjected to a multitude of horrific sights accompanied by the use of sound until it is deemed he has been vanquished of his wrathful ideals and can re-enter society.

On leaving prison Alex's mind is in dilemma, the violence now surrounding him in a world of his own creating leads his thoughts to be pulled towards his newly required passivity as a result of the Ludovico technique, and towards his old ways of the joyous revelling in chaos and wrath.

MOBY-DICK; OR, THE WHALE
HERMAN MELVILLE

In the portrayal of a soul's total emersion within wrath, Herman Melville's 1851 novel 'Moby-Dick; or The Whale' depicts its character, Captain Ahab, as a man consumed with the rage and vengeance identified with the deadly sin.

Taken from the author's own experience aboard a whaling ship in the early 1840's and from true accounts of a white sperm whale named Mocha Dick which was killed off the coast of Chile near Mocha island, the story is narrated by Ishmael, the only survivor of the ill-fated whaling ship the Pequod. The young seaman tells the tale of is captain and crew's battle against the great white whale Moby Dick. Having lost his leg to the whale on a previous encounter, Captain Ahab's self-destructive obsessive anger to the beast leads him to willing sacrifice not only his crew but also his own life in his hunt for revenge against Moby Dick.

As Ahab's excessive wrath deepens, Ishmael observes the sin and its total empowerment over his captain who will stop at nothing in his single pursuit of killing his nemesis.

THE FIFTH HEAVENLY VIRTUE

PATIENCE

Noun: patience / ˈpeɪʃ(ə)ns/
An ability to accept or endure problems with no annoyance.
"His patience in matters was to be admired, if not heeded."
Synonyms: forbearance, tolerance, restraint, self-restraint,
resignation, stoicism, fortitude, sufferance, endurance.

'Patience is bitter, but its fruit is sweet.'

Jean-Jacques Rousseau

An Introduction to Patience

As Wrath's nemesis, patience is regarded as dissolving the overpowering emotions of rage and fury, and eradicating any thoughts of vengeance towards another soul which may be harbouring within an individual.

Examples of the Heavenly virtue of patience can be seen in literature and art as well as in theological and mythological writings.

It was Salacia the Roman personification of Patience and Forbearance who enlisted her powers of patience to subdue her husband Neptune in his sometimes wrathful delight of producing the stormy seas so feared by seafarers of the Mediterranean.

In the Christian Church, the Apostle Paul would symbolise the values of having patience in a believer's life by identifying fortitude as one of the nine Holy Fruits of the Holy Spirit.

These instances of patience and the qualities of which are found within are created to gain an understanding towards the much valued quality within an individual's soul.

The importance of having patience of heart is stressed in the Mahayana tradition of Buddhism where patience is observed as being the third precept of the six Paramita and continues its influence within the first of the foundations of the Buddhist doctrine 'The Four Noble Truths'.

Hindu scripture also speaks of the importance of patience. Portrayed in the ten Pariksha, these codes of conduct towards attaining patience are viewed as being of the upmost importance for a soul following the faith of Hinduism.

As can be seen, the fifth Heavenly virtue of patience is an integral characteristic needed in attaining not only peace in life but as is found in the religions of Asia, as a step towards gaining enlightenment of being.

PATIENCE IN RELIGION

CHRISTIANITY

'But if we hope for what we do not see, we wait for it with patience.'
Galatians 6: 9

Taken from the Latin - longanimitas, patience and forbearance in the Christian Church is neither identified as one of the three virtues or as being part of one of the more traditional Cardinal virtues.

Within Christian theology it would be the apostle Paul who would recognise the qualities of a soul applying patience in their daily lives. This would lead him to including the virtue as being one of the fruits of the Holy Spirit, the mention of which was included in Paul's message to the Galatians.

'Love, joy, peace, patience, kindness, goodness, faithfulness, gentleness and self-control. Against such things there is no law'.
Galatians 5: 21-23

Observed as nine qualities in which to aid a Christian's life and so allowing entry into the Kingdom of Heaven, it is believed that the moment those who allow God into their life shall receive the Holy Spirit. This acceptance leads the Holy Spirit to transform a new believer's life by bestowing to them the opportunity of tasting His Holy Fruits.

Sometimes depicted in the form of actual fruits to aid further understanding in a new covert, patience is often portrayed as a pineapple or a pear to symbolise the sweetness of taste when following the intricacies of holding and practicing patience in an individual's life.

HINDUISM

'Patience is subjugating the senses.'
The Mahabharata

With impatience and wrath regarded as major vices amongst devotees of Hinduism, patience is considered an indispensable virtue towards finding peace of mind and a step towards finding understanding for the misguided actions of others.

A Hindu who has mastered the qualities of patience are viewed as having the ability to withstand contrasting matters such as sorrow and happiness, heartache and love, disquiet and peace of mind. In gaining these abilities a want for retribution against another's soul for any misdeeds directed to the practitioner of patience is therefore eradicated, both in actions and that of thought.

In the philosophy of the physical and mental practices of Yoga, Hinduism recognises that there are ten foundations of patience that if followed will lead an individual to gaining patience and the tolerance of others in their life. Known as the 'Ten Pariksaha' (patience and tolerance) these guidelines offer a devotee a code of conduct to live by in the want of attaining patience:

Saucha - the spiritual cleansing of the body and of the mind in the quest for self-identification and knowledge of the soul.
Arjava – to be truthful in deeds towards others in speaking or of thought.
Asteya – not to desire that which belongs to another.
Brahmacharya – remaining unattached in mind and body.
Daya – to bestow kindness and compassion onto all sentient beings encountered.
Mitahara – refraining from overindulgence in matters of food, drink and a want of wealth.
Kshama – an acceptance of others sometimes harmful acts directed at the self.
Satya – always being truthful.
Ahimsa – to not hold or utilse anger or violence onto others, either physically of in thought.
Dhriti – to not dwell on loss, be it that of wealth or in relationship matters of family, friends or romantic relationships.

Regarded as a refined theme throughout the sacred texts of the Bhagavad Gita, an emphasis on the practice of meditation is portrayed as one path towards gaining patience, which in turn will lead a devotee to experience stillness of mind and allow entry into an overwhelming state of tranquillity.

BUDDHISM

'Patience is the key. Remember, a jug fills drop by drop.'
Gautama Buddha

Patience in the Tibetan Mahayana Buddhist tradition is observed as the third of the six 'Paramitas' a list of perfections for a soul to attain in want of achieving enlightenment. These perfections are:

Dana - the generosity and the act of giving the self to another.
Sil - good morals, correct actions to others and self-control.
Ksanti - patience, fortitude, the acceptance and tolerance of others.
Virya - to have diligence, verve and vitality in life.
Dhyana – contemplation, attentiveness and focus.
Prajna – knowledge, wisdom and an insight into the workings of the world.

It is the third Ksanti Paramita that represents the need for patience in an individual's life, which in mastering brings forth the qualities of forbearance moderation and leniency.

Observed by the Buddha as representing the patience in the acceptance of other's acts towards the self or towards another, this acceptance begins with the understanding and implementation of the first of the Four Noble Truths, the truth of Dukka.

In the acknowledgment that life contains suffering, the application of Ksanti leads to the acknowledgment that life contains suffering and so guides the devotee onwards towards the succeeding three Noble Truths, and the path leading to escaping the cycle of reincarnation and continued suffering of mind.

In the avoidance of any situation that may bring emotional pain or physical discomfort, this is seen as an individual not utilising Ksanti and protecting themselves from harm.

As Buddhism designates patience as the endurance of any such difficult circumstances, by renouncing and hiding away from these situations an individual is turning their back on Ksanti by not submitting to its ways of patience and the endurance of life's problems.

In an individual's grasping that there really is no 'self' to protect, and that the concept of who or what said individual represents is a result of the ego, then the perception of discomfort alters in the realisation that pain cannot exist as there is no 'self' to receive it. This leads an individual to understanding and employing the paramita of Prajna, and so results in the exploration of the remaining four paramitas.

PATIENCE IN MYTHOLOGY

GREEK

Daughter of Prince Icarius of Sparta and Periboea, the Naiad Nymph (female spirit of Fresh Water) of Lakonia, Penelope's devotion towards her husband, the Grecian heroic figure Odysseus, led her to being the representation of patience in ancient Greek mythology.

Penelope's other attributes of faithfulness and intelligence were displayed in her fortitude of waiting for Odysseus to return from his twenty year journey and battles in the Trojan War. This patience was amplified by her avoidance of marriage to over one hundred suitors during this time.

On Odysseus' return he disguised himself as an old beggar and on meeting Penelope finds she has remained faithful to him.

Penelope sees through her husband's disguise but does not tell of her discovery and instead asks the old beggar to take part in a contest of skill alongside her many other suitors, the winner of which will receive her hand.

With a competition of bowman ship where each suitor must first string Odysseus' and then shoot an arrow through several axe heads, Penelope watches each of her suitors fail until the old beggar achieves the trial.

Unveiling himself as her husband, Odysseus kills all the suitors, yet he can still not convince his wife that it is he. Penelope's suspicions are in that the man before him claiming to be her husband may be one of the Gods disguised as Odysseus, so she sets another task.

Asking her servants to reposition her and her husband's marital bed, Penelope knows that only the true Odysseus would know their beds exact position having it been he who built their bed from their home's surrounding olive trees.

On recognising the new position of the bed it is revealed to Penelope that her husband now truly stands before her and after two decades of waiting patiently for Odysseus they are finally reunited.

ROMAN

In Roman mythology it is Salacia who is seen as the Goddess of the Seas and Oceans, with 'Sal' translating salt in Latin. It was through her affinity with these waters that she would also personify the virtue of patience.

Wife of Neptune, God of Sea, Ocean and Water, Salacia's attributes of patience and fortitude are accredited to her grace and good nature which are displayed in her marriage to the sometimes tempestuous God of the Sea.

In her actions of emitting patience as Neptune's Queen, sailors looked upon Salacia as representing the ocean when at its calmest and in its stillness during the closing hours of sunlight.

Throughout history, Salacia's physical appearance has been depicted as standing beside her husband on a giant pearl shell chariot drawn by numerous sea creatures from turtles to dolphins to sea horses, her beautiful form crowned by a halo of seaweed.

In this position it is portrayed that out on the open seas it is Salacia's patience and calmness which subdues Neptune's often stormy temperament.

PATIENCE IN ART AND LITERATURE

ALLEGORY OF PATIENCE
CARLO DOLCI

Carlo Dolci's Baroque style 1877 oval shaped painting Allegory of Patience, portrays a young woman, her shoulders bare and draped in dark brown robing which is contrasted by her revealing low cropped orange underclothing.

Predominantly based in Florence, Italy, Dolci's choice of using a young woman whose beauty as reminiscent of the times, was in order to convey patience as the concept of unrequited love; that of a soul's want for another's reply of similar emotional intensity.

With the model's hands crossed just above her waist line symbolising a lessening of chastity, her features express a culmination of love for another and a subtle hint of anxiousness as to what her answers shall be towards romantic conclusions.

PATIENCE ON A MONUMENT SMILING AT GRIEF
JOHN RODDAM SPENCER STANHOPE

William Shakespeare's tragi-comedy Twelfth Night provided Stanhope with inspiration for his early 1880's painting, where in the fourth scene of the play's second act Viola says to Orsino;

"She sat like patience on a monument. Smiling at grief. Was this not love indeed?"

The composition of Stanhope's piece depicts two figures representing the embodiment of Patience and Grief in a garden of ancient Greek white marble statues. A seated Patience rests her head on her hand and smiles down to Grief kneeling at her feet.

Grief is portrayed as a beautiful brunette woman draped in colourful robes as was prominent in the Pre-Raphaelite style of which Stanhope belonged.

The juxtaposition of both figure's hands plays an important role, as where Grief covers her eyes Patience looks to her companion displaying a knowing of the need for waiting and perseverance when shrouded in life's sometimes problems and heartaches.

THE DIVINE COMEDY: PURGATORIO
DANTE ALIGHIERI

In Purgatorio, the second part of Dante Alighieri's 'The Divine Comedy', it is the third terrace of the Wrathful where Dante encounters patience.

Guided by the poet Virgil, both meet with the souls who were shrouded with wrath throughout their lives. Listening to accounts of wrathful deeds and acts of anger, Dante begins to understand the torment of what both inner and outer traits of wrath entail. Virgil leads Dante from such tales of fury and vengeance to where an individual is purged of the sin of wrath.

Shown how patience cures all anger in the form of becoming a peacemaker, Dante recognises how the virtue of patience is a vital characteristic if tranquillity and amity in a soul's life is to be attained.

WACVIE,
FAITH BANDLER

The Australian civil rights activist of Scottish and Indian heritage, Faith Bandler, portrays the virtue of patience within her 1977 biographical novel Wacvie.

A fictionalised account of the life of her father Wacvie Mussingkon, Bandler tells of how at the age of thirteen he was kidnapped from a village on the south pacific island of Vanuatu and then sold as a slave to work on Australia's east coast sugar plantations.

It is in the circumstances of being a slave and under another's total command that Wacvie's view on his position invites patience into his heart.

The patience shown by the boy slave is told in the metaphor of approaching storm clouds, where with patience and release of any anxiety resting within the soul, it is known that the tempest shall at one time pass and so reveal blue skies once more.

The Sixth Deadly Sin

ENVY

Noun: envy / ˈɛnvi/
A resentful longing aroused by someone else's possessions, qualities, or luck.
"She was resentful and held great envy to what he had and was."
Synonyms: jealousy, enviousness, covetousness, desire
resentment, resentfulness, bitterness, discontent.

'The wicked envy and hate; it is their way of admiring.'

Victor Hugo

AN INTRODUCTION TO ENVY

In the desire for what another holds, be it wealth, lifestyle or position in life, Envy bestows its victim with the added malady of experiencing emotional torment on hearing of someone else's good fortune. The harbouring of envy leads to a bitterness that burrows deep within the soul and is seen as one of the major causes of suffering in the world.

So embedded in the characteristic traits of humanity, the Catholic Church not only includes envy as a Cardinal sin, but also recognises its influence in the Ten Commandments and the act of coveting thy neighbour's wife. Seen as an unwholesome mental factor in Tibetan Buddhism, the term Irshya is observed in describing envy, and placed alongside the ranks of rage, fury, resentment and spitefulness.

Hinduism also perceives envy as an abomination of the soul and recognises how a devotee's mind can become clouded of judgement and lost within the mire of wanting what another has in ways of possessions, intelligence and luck. Although envy and jealousy are inevitably connected in the sense of bringing pain and suffering into an individual's life, the two hold different features.

With envy being seen as experiencing emotional pain in the lack of what another has and directing ill will towards the receiver of good fortune, jealousy is experienced when a risk emerges of losing that of which is held dear to an individual. This is more commonly realised in the interaction of romantic situations.

This fear that something gained will be taken away signifies jealousy, and although this can bring suffering to an individual's wellbeing, the emotions of envy run a little deeper, bringing discord and strife into the heart of a soul undergoing the sour taste of envy.

For an individual under envy's sway, it is almost inconceivable to them to see that by striving towards achieving to attain what another has succeeded in gaining, the suffering associated with envy is subdued. By cultivating the motivation of reaching a similar position of the one who envy is directed towards, the burning emotions of the sin ebb away, leaving the one once consumed by the sin to gain not only a similar standing of riches or spiritual progression, but also some self-respect for themselves, in that they have succeeded in both achieving and also that they no longer play victimhood to the lack of motivation envious people habitually hold within them.

ENVY IN RELIGION

BUDDHISM

'Do not overrate what you have received nor envy others. He who envies others does not obtain peace of mind.'
Gautama Buddha

Within Buddhist tradition envy or jealousy are defined under the term of 'Irshya'. Derived from the Pali word Issa and translated in the Tibet Mahayana branch of Buddhism as 'tradok', Irshya is identified as an individual who while being highly motivated to achieve wealth and material items and the respect of others cannot bear to see someone else achieve that of which they themselves strive for.

Irshya is seen as one of the 'Twenty Secondary Unwholesome Mental Factors' in the Mahayana tradition. These precepts are found in the third century BC teachings of the Abhidharma of Buddhist theology and are broken down into five sections of a fifty one mental factor list.

The Five Universal Mental Factors
The Five Object-Determining Mental Factors
The Eleven Virtuous Mental Factors
The Six Root Unwholesome Factors
The Twenty Secondary Unwholesome Factors
The Four Changeable Mental Factors

Irshya is placed fifth behind rage, resentment, concealment and spitefulness in the 'Twenty Secondary Unwholesome Mental Factors'.

The Buddhist concept of attachment is observed as being a factor within a soul harbouring envy.

By conveying envy or jealousy towards another for their achievements, be them of material or spiritual gains, an individual can at times exaggerate the success of others in their mind when comparing their own life to those who have succeeded in attaining what is desired.

In the actions of an individual comparing themselves to another attachment of the ego comes forth and so lays blind the understanding that there is no 'me' and so enhances the suffering of the individual under the influence of Irshya. This can in effect also bring suffering to the one of whom envy and jealousy are focused towards.

In Tibetan Buddhism envy is represented by the horse, as when with other horses it holds great displeasure if another horse is running faster than they. This equates to humanity's drive for position in the world and a similar running to achieve coupled with the distaste of another's often deserved accomplishments.

The antidote for envy is kindness. This is achieved, and so ridding a devotee of envy, in using kindness as a focus in meditation as well as cultivating the virtue in carrying out acts of kindness and generosity to others.

CHRISTIANITY

'And I saw that all toil and all achievement spring from one person's envy of another. This too is meaningless, a chasing after the wind.'
Ecclesiastes 4: 4 - 16

In The Roman Catholic Church, envy is recognised as being one of the most heinous of all the seven deadly sins.

Given the censure of being included as one of the Cardinal sins, medieval theologian Thomas Aquinas would say of the sin of envy:

'Envy according to the aspect of its object is contrary to charity, whence the soul derives its spiritual life... Charity rejoices in our neighbour's good, while envy grieves over it.'

Observed as the punishment given to a soul that has spent a lifetime wallowing in the mire of envy, the Catholic Church's view is that in living such actions the sinner is resigned to spend the rest of eternity in either pools of freezing water or alternatively in some beliefs held within the Church, bathing in fire and brimstone within the depths of Hell.

The Church of England views the reasoning behind humanity's transgression of envy is from an individual's constant comparison to others. Questioning if another soul is better than themselves in ways of attractiveness, intelligence or even luck, leads only to a false admiration in which envy is subtly hidden behind the enquirers mind. For if envy was not present then there would be no need for an individual to even consider if another's attributes are greater than their own.

In theological terms, envy first appeared in the Book of Genesis when Cain took it upon himself to murder his brother, Abel.

It would be Cain's envy towards his brother which saw to him being the first to commit murder. Resulting from God showing Abel as being His favoured soul, Cain's envy consumed every part of him. So overcome was he in the emotions created by the power of envy he committed the homicidal act upon his brother.

The sons of Adam and Eve who were both created by God, with Cain being born before Abel, the Bible specifies that Cain was the first of humankind to be born unto the world and Able the first to die upon it.

The Bible also tells of how it was envy towards God that instigated the fall of angels from Heaven and so denoting that the masters of damnation are in fact partakers of envy's traits.

The Church talks of envy as being the bleakest of sins, for what joy can be found in experiencing mental torture and pain when hearing tributes of the achievements of another's soul?

The characteristics of envy are many, and as identified by the Catholic Church, inherent in all souls.

With being such a strong driving force in life in terms of the want of the success some attain yet is often eluded in others, envy can be seen as being a hard sin to find any release from.

Christianity's observations of finding salvation from envy are many and range from acts of emulation and imitation to forgiveness of the individual's own soul for the indiscretions that are directed at another, all these actions of which are believed to be aided by God's grace.

HINDUISM

Those who are envious and mischievous, who are the lowest among men, are cast by Me into the ocean of material existence.'
The Bhagavad Gita Chapter 16: Verse 19

In Hinduism it is regarded that Karma holds a key towards the release of an individual suffering from the envy of others.

Envy or jealousy directed at another can be overcome when the sinner looks to those who have what is desired to them and recognises that those who are the focus of their envy have gained such riches from good Karmic actions carried out in past lifetimes.

It is in this understanding that a Hindu devotee can release any ill will to others that is generated by the sin of envy.

Observed as an unwholesome characteristic within humanity, Hinduism states that becoming lost in jealousy results in the mind becoming clouded and off balance when focused on the selfish want of another's position or wealth in life.

This loss of focus is further frowned upon as said envious individual in turn does little if nothing to advance their own life so they too may also achieve what another has, and instead continues to direct misgivings towards those who the sinner assumes does not deserve what they have achieved in their lifetime.

These concerns of envy and jealousy are one of many themes found in the Hindu text of The Bhagavad Gita, one instance of which Lord Krishna says;

'One who does not envy but is a compassionate friend to all... such a devotee is very dear to me.'
The Bhagavad Gita

ENVY IN MYTHOLOGY

GREEK

The personified spirit of Envy and Jealousy, Phthonus, concentrated his attributes on bequeathing envy onto mortals who were either in the throes of passion or entwined in the emotions of love and devotion.

The son of Dionysus, God of Wine and Fertility, and Nyx, Goddess and embodiment of the Night, Phthonus married a multitude of women only to kill each one of them in suspicion of their infidelity to him.

Phthonus' aptitude on bestowing envious thoughts onto not only mortals but also the Gods would see him linked closely with

Nemesis, the Goddess of Retribution and the Reprisal of those who receive undeserved wealth.

In Greek mythology Nemesis, like Phthonus, is concerned with the matter of love relationships. Drawn towards themes of romance between mortals it is said that Nemesis played a hand in instigating the Trojan War between the Achaeans and the Spartans.

Her actions to prompt the ensuing ten year battle were not only from her implied influence of bringing about Helen and Paris' adulterous affair, but also in turn it was Nemesis who pointed a finger as Helen's unfaithfulness in her marriage to Menelaus, the Mycenaean king of Sparta, and so revealing her and Paris' infatuation with one another.

ROMAN

Invidia, the Roman Goddess of Retribution, Vengeance and Envy is seen as being a counterpart of Nemesis. Said to have had a poisoned tongue and with one glare could inflict ill will onto her observers, Invidia's physical description is of having discoloured teeth, soft pale skin and being the holder of a lithe, slim body.

It was not until medieval times that Christianity secured Invidia and her wicked ways to represent the deadly sin of envy, and although keeping her lean body, she was portrayed as having a snake wrapped around her waist, its head raised up and biting into her heart. This was to symbolise envy's trait of bitterness consuming its internal self.

Selfishness if also accredited to Invidia and is depicted in Biblical art works of the Middle Ages as having her one hand raised to her mouth, representing that the ancient Roman personification of envy holds no consideration for another's wellbeing and cares only for herself.

Featured in both Roman and Greek mythology, Cerberus, the 'Hound of Hades', was also connected with Invidia and her equal Nemesis. The three headed dog that stood guard at the gates of the Underworld to prevent the dead from leaving was believed in medieval times to be the embodiment of Invidia, with each of its three heads representing a characteristic of Invidia deceitful traits ascribed to envy and reckoning.

Envy in Art and Literature

Envy
Giotto

Giotto di Bondone, the fourteenth century painter created a series of works dedicated to portraying the seven vices in the style of his times.

Painted in 1303 and originally titled Invidia after the Roman personification of Envy, in his depiction of envy Giotto represents the sin as a large eared elderly woman. With the addition of horns and a serpent slithering from her month, its head raised as to meet with the old crone eye to eye, Giotto placed envy standing in a ball of flames. Symbolising an individual who is under the envy's influence, the flames licking up the old woman's legs represent the internal fire experienced by the sinner. This metaphor is enhanced by the bag of money held tight within her grasp.

Jealousy
Edvard Munch

Painted in 1895 by Norwegian artist Edvard Munch, Jealousy took the Biblical theme of the Garden of Eden and transferred the setting to parallel the emotional turmoil present in his own personal life.

To the left of the painting, Munch's friend the Polish poet Przybyszewski is shown from the chest up as a solemn colourless character whilst in the background behind him two figures stand beneath an apple tree.

The two figures, one a featureless man the other a nude woman with a red cloak draped from her shoulders, look to one another as the woman reaches up to pick one of the forbidden fruits above them. Depicting his friend as jealousy, it is surmised that the featureless man so enamoured by the naked woman is Munch himself and the woman is Przybyszewski wife.

Painting the same composition over ten times for the remainder of his life, Munch's passionate obsession towards the piece was fuelled by his presumed romantic entanglement with his friend's wife.

This gives reason for Munch's portrayal of Przybyszewski as a low-spirited and disenchanted husband aware of his wife's infidelity.

OTHELLO
(THE TRAGEDY OF OTHELLO, THE MOOR OF VENICE)
WILLIAM SHAKESPEARE

Shakespeare's tragedy of envy, love, lust, jealousy and betrayal centres on the deceitful characteristics of Iago and his envious plans to obtain what he desires through the deception and manipulation of his friend Othello, the Moor general of the Venetian army.

Becoming an ensign to Othello, Iago instigates a deep friendship between him and his general. In finding kinship with Othello, Iago then uses his skills of emotional manipulation and deception to convince Othello that his wife, Desdemona, is being unfaithful to him.

Sending Othello in a fury at such news, Iago watches his plans take shape as his general becomes lost within envy and jealousy and is filled with all the essences the sin promotes.

THE GREAT GATSBY
F. SCOTT FITZGERALD

The Great Gatsby, F. Scott Fitzgerald's 1925 novella, is a study of one man's envy which in due course leads to obsession.

When Nick Carraway, a young man form the mid-west of America, becomes fascinated with his neighbour Jay Gatsby, he uncovers that behind Jay's charismatic personality and lavish lifestyle he lead with the nouveau rich of Long Island, that the man who appears to have it all is in fact tormented within envy's grip.

Envy and jealousy are also played out amongst Fitzgerald's characters surrounding Gatsby, most notably in the complex union of husband and wife Tom and Daisy Buchanan.

It is Tom's mistress, Myrtle who displays envy towards another's position in life, as although she may receive money and gifts from Tom, being of a lower class she looks to her lover's wife Daisy with great envy and the luxurious existence Myrtle herself aspires to.

Although portraying envy within situations of adultery, The Great Gatsby's theme of envy is focused on that of Jay and Daisy's emotional interplay.

With Jay and Daisy's past history being one as former lovers, Nick discovers that when Jay left to fight in the war he and Daisy vowed to reunite on his return. As Daisy's wait continued into years her need for affection grew too strong and she married Tom, a fact of which Jay discovered on his return to America.

Determined to win Daisy back and conquer his envy towards his love's husband, Jay hopes to capture Daisy's heart through his lavish and at times ostentatious lifestyle.

Throughout the book the intricate world of the rich and their jealous and envious traits are unveiled in acts of injustice and infidelity. The sins of greed and lust are prevalent too in keeping with the concept of envy as a running focus amongst Long Island's elite classes, yet it is the young Midwesterner who undoubtedly shows envy at its height, captured in his subtle masking of the obsessional interest he holds and his desire for what is seen, lived and the position held in life by the Great Jay Gatsby.

KINDNESS

Noun: kindness / ˈkīn(d)nəs /
The quality of being generous and considerate.
"He thanked them all for their kindness."
Synonyms: kind heartedness, affection, warmth, gentleness,
concern, care, thoughtfulness, selflessness, compassion, sympathy.

*'When we feel love and kindness toward others, it not only makes others feel loved
and cared for, but it helps us also to develop inner happiness and peace.'*

His Holiness the 14th Dalai Lama

An Introduction to Kindness

Often greeted with suspicion, the Heavenly virtue of Kindness is seldom talked of, yet its ability to heal the suffering found in the heart of an individual under the influence of one of the deadly sins is unsurpassed, be them either an instigator or victim from another's transgressions

An example of this is how a sufferer of the sin of wrath views the kind actions of another. Smothered in rage both internally and outwardly, kindness is seen to them as being a weakness and not for the strength it truly is. For to selflessly give to another without any want in return, be it in ways of love or philanthropy, commands the greatest of power held within the soul, much more so than the weakness of allowing anger and fury to reside within the heart. This inevitably leads to bitterness, which if left unresolved results in a lifetime of suffering due to the avoidance and the pushing away of any type of kindness shown to them by others.

Kindness and the values held therein is an integral feature of all world religions.

The central aspect of Buddhism, the qualities of kindness are portrayed in the context of compassion, of which without, the fundamental belief of Buddhist scripture cannot be adhered to.

In Hinduism, the importance of kindness is in the belief that God Himself is the embodiment of kindness, and that through practicing meditation a Hindu can reach the heights of Divine ecstasy, most notably in the performance of the nine forms of Bhakti Yogic practice.

Christianity also holds great reverence to the heavenly virtue. Kindness can be found within the nine 'Holy Fruits' as told by the Apostle Paul.

In cultivating and performing acts of kindness in life and thought, a dissolving of each of the deadly sins occurs. This puts kindness at the forefront of the seven Heavenly virtues.

Bringing with it a sense of peace and contentment, these states are reached when administering kindness to others, although there is another facet of attaining said peace of mind. This is found when an individual shows not only kindness to others but also to themselves and allowing compassion into their heart and eventually their soul on journey along its spiritual path.

KINDNESS IN RELIGION

BUDDHISM

'Kindness should become the natural way of life, not the exception.'
Gautama Buddha

Kindness is one of the core elements of the Buddhist belief system and is the fundamental basis of all teaching within Buddhism; for without kindness there would be no compassion, forgiveness or reverence for others.

In showing love and kindness to all sentient beings and displaying the same loving kindness to ourselves and our own soul, these actions are recognised as 'Metta', the ancient Pali word denoting benevolence, good will, kindness and having a genuine joy and interest in the wellbeing and happiness of others.

In the Tibetan Mahayana tradition of Buddhism, Metta is identified as being part of Brahmavihara meditation. Consisting of four precepts of which to live by, these act as a guide of instruction for a devotee to attain kindness and so administer such good will to others.

Known as the 'Four Immeasurables', it is believed that in cultivating and achieving the principles of Metta leads its practitioner to receive rebirth into the kingdom of Brahma, the creator God and the one who encouraged the Buddha to tell others of the knowledge he had gained after his attainment of enlightenment.

The Brahmavihara are regarded as being the 'homes of Brahma', with each of its four concepts representing a different feature of the states of kindness. These are:

Loving-kindness – Metta
The action of transmitting peace, good will and happiness to all living beings.
Compassion – Karuna
An action derived from Metta in that the suffering and pain of others is identified as being the practitioner of the Brahma sutra's own.
Empathetic joy – Mudita
The action of finding happiness in seeing joy resides in others,

recognised in the knowledge that the practitioner did nothing in influencing such joy.

Equanimity – Upeksa

The action of holding tranquillity of heart, and the treating of all others with fairness and with no judgement, prejudice or bias towards them.

Kindness and compassion can be seen today in the physical sense by the presence of Jetsun Jamphel Ngawang Lobsang Yeshe Tenzin Gyatso, or as he is usually known, His Holiness the 14th Dalai Lama.

Following the Gulug school of Tibetan Buddhism, the Dalai Lama, whose title derives for the Tibetan/Mongolian words for ocean (Dalai) and teacher (Lama), is the successor in the lineage of Tulkus who are reincarnations of the Bodhisattva of Compassion, Avalokitesvara, seen as the embodiment of compassion in all Buddhas.

Observed in Mahayana Buddhism, a Bodhisattva is a spiritually advanced Buddhist devotee who although being able to reach Nirvana decides to remain on Earth as to aid those in suffering with his compassion.

As with the present and the previous Dalai Lamas and the ones to follow, kindness proves a foundation to Buddhist teaching and plays an important role in the lives of those who follow the Buddha and adhere to his teachings.

CHRISTIANITY

'Put on then, as God's chosen ones, holy and beloved, compassionate hearts, kindness, humility, meekness, and patience.'
Colossians 3: 12

In the eyes of the Christian Church, Kindness is a Heavenly virtue if when administered correctly denotes the action of providing something pleasant from the heart to another without want of anything in return.

This definition of the act of kindness is described as showing benevolence and generosity to others, even when those others may at times exercise the believer's patience.

It would be the Apostle Paul who would identify the qualities and hence the Heavenly virtue of kindness in the ninth book of the New Testament with his Letter to the Galatians.

In Paul's message to the Galatians, his want of instilling the word of God to others and the faith held within Christianity, he used an example of the church's beliefs of 'The Fruit of the Holy Spirit', a Biblical term used for describing the nine traits for a Christian to follow in life and so resulting in stepping closer to God's side.

'But the fruit of the Spirit is love, joy, peace, patience, kindness, goodness, faithfulness, gentleness, self-control.'
Galatians 5: 22-23

The kindness found in the fifth category of Paul's doctrine, confirms the correct moral standings surrounding the concept of kindness, wherein the meeting of others needs is stressed but must also be overseen with the absence of malice.

In the Catholic Church, The Fruit of the Holy Spirit is equated in the 'The Vulgate', St. Jerome's fourth century Latin version of the Bible that became popular within Catholicism in the early sixteenth century.

The Vulgate extends Paul's precepts of nine fruits into that of twelve fruits, these being: charity, joy, peace, patience, kindness, goodness, generosity, gentleness, faithfulness, modesty, self-control, chastity.

Be them nine or twelve, both factions of the Church looks to believers in hope that each shall ask for God's forgiveness in their transgressions, and so follow the virtues of moral ethics found in the Holy Fruits.

This in turn will empower the members of their congregation through the faith held in the Holy Spirit, and so by attaining kindness in life and portraying kindness towards others, they may enjoy the abundance of earthly delights of which God has created for them.

HINDUISM

'Compassion is kindness to all living beings especially when they are in distress. Non-covetousness is self-satisfaction with what one has been allotted in life.'
The Bhagavad Gita

Hinduism portrays Kindness as being a God like quality as a Hindu believes that God is the embodiment of kindness.

The importance of the upkeep and cultivation of kindness in daily life extends further than just performing the virtue itself. Various meditation practices are promoted as a way of advancing kindness within a devotee, one of which is found in the Yogic practice of Bhakti.

An ancient Sanskrit word meaning the devotion, love and worship towards any God or Deity to which such actions are directed, Bhakti is observed as being one of the many spiritual paths taken towards the attainment of enlightenment.

Having nine forms of practice, Bhakti's structure of devotion to a Divine entity includes the worship of a particular image, a focus of the mind upon Lord Vishnu the Supreme Divinity, the singing of devotional mantras or verse and the a whole surrender of the soul to the Divine.

To further a connection with God or with Gods, as in many other Asian religions, Hinduism supports the meditation technique of Japa.

Performed in either a seated position or when walking, Japa involves the repetition of a particular mantra, a sentence or word that holds spiritual powers and is personal to its orator.

In the Hindu practice Japa is used as an additional aid in the progress of an individual's spiritual journey, both in this lifetime and the subsequent ones following.

With kindness being a major theme in the Holy text of the Bhagavad Gita, Bhakti and its qualities of kindness was also revered by the Hindu spiritual teacher of the nineteenth and the twentieth century, and advocate of Yogic practice, Sivananda Saraswati, who said of Bhakti:

Bhakti softens the heart and removes jealousy, hatred, lust, anger egoism, pride and arrogance. It infuses joy, Divine ecstasy, bliss, peace and knowledge.'
Sivananda Saraswati

KINDNESS IN MYTHOLOGY

GREEK

Gaining her title from combining the Greek words for friendship and lovers (philos) and combining them with that of thought and mind (phrenos), Philophrosyne, or 'friendly thoughts', is regarded as the Greek Goddess of Kindness, to which the ancient Grecian society would call upon when the essence of good hospitality and welcomes were needed in their home.

Also seen as the personified spirit of Salutations and Amiable company, it would be observed that alongside her three sisters Euthenia, Eupheme and Eucleia, Philophrosyne attributions of friendliness towards others matched her sister's similar kind characteristics of prosperous luck, praise and acclamation, and the holding of good reputation.

Daughter of Hephaestus, the Greek God of artists and those who follow creative pursuits, and the Goddess of Beauty and Majesty, Aglaea, Philophrosyne's lineage reached the height of Greek mythological characters with King and Queen of the Gods Zeus and Hera heralded as being her grandparents.

Aglaea, the mother of Philophrosyne, is classed as the youngest of the three Graces, or Charites. Together with her companions Euphrosyne, the Goddess of Joy and Merriment and Thalia the Goddess of Celebration and Rejoicing, Aglaea introduced her four daughters to the feasts and festivities of the Gods, resulting in Philophrosyne, Euthenia, Eupheme and Eucleia becoming recognised as Mount Olympus' younger Charites.

Elements of Philophrosyne's qualities can be identified in daily life in the acceptance of others encountered in daily life. In using the Goddess' traits of kindness and friendliness this in effect can entice others to reciprocate her virtues and so illuminate any of the harshness that at times are chanced upon when meeting another soul.

It is in Philophrosyne's ability to display her hospitality in the act of kindness towards others that shows what being kind really is. Yet, if hostility is still met with in another upon the presenting kindness to them, this is where Philophrosyne's talents truly come into play. In these moments, the Goddess of Kindness holds her dignity and in turn employs her qualities in that of leading by example.

ROMAN

In Roman mythology it seen that the Goddess of Light and aider of Childbirth, Lucina, holds the attributes of kindness within her many qualities.

Represented in ancient Roman antiquities as having long plaited light coloured hair she is often depicted seated with her son, Mars resting on her lap.

It would be the birth of Lucina's son that symbolised kindness of the heart, for in repayment of the kindness shown to her by the Goddess of Flowers and the emergence of Springtime, Flora, who aided Lucina to conceive her child alone with the help of enchanted fauna. This led to Lucina to be known as the protector of pregnant women and of those in the act of childbirth.

These attributes also expanded Lucina's influence of the maternal, in that she would be called upon by the women of ancient Rome who had trouble conceiving and were desperate for a child of their own.

KINDNESS IN ART AND LITERATURE

PRIMAVERA
SANDRO BOTTICELLI

Symbolism of kindness abounds throughout Sandro Botticelli's 1482 masterpiece, the 'Primavera'.

Also known as the 'Allegory of Spring', the Italian Renaissance artist depicts the qualities and values of benevolence and goodwill through the actions of the nine sentient beings represented in the emergence of spring, in what is believed by some art historians as being a depiction of Dante Alighieri's interpretation of the Garden of Eden from his epic saga The Divine Comedy.

Standing in the centre of the painting, Venus, the Roman Goddess of Love and Beauty looks to her observer with kindness, as does the Roman Goddess of Flowers, Flora, represented as the blonde female figure to the viewer's right of Venus.

As Flora emits kindness through the scattering of flowers and seeds onto the grasslands beneath her, this act is interpreted in giving others joy in seeing seeds bloom. This is shown by the multitude of different flowers at the feet of all present within the painting.

Standing beside Flora, the Nymph Chloris, looks back to her loved one, the Roman God of the West winds, Zephyrus, her close affiliation to Flora coming about from her transforming the mythical characters of Narcissus, Crocus and Hyacinthus into flowers.

To the far left of the Primavera stands Mercury, the Roman God of Travellers, Luck and writers of Script and Poetry. Mercury also represents those who partake in the world of commerce, hence his name being holding a faint link to the Latin, merchandise.

Standing tall, his right arm raises high above him where in his hand he holds a caduceus, a short staff with two snakes twisting around its handle, and is said to ward off any approaching storms, a kindness much needed in the onset of spring after a harsh winter.

Between Mercury and Venus, the three Graces, Aglaea, the mother of Philophrosyne, and her companions Euphrosyne, Thalia, stand forming a circle, a hand held in one another's to complete the union. As two of the Charites hold their hands aloft towards the branches bearing fruit above them, a hovering Cupid, the God of Desire and affection and reputed son of Venus, looks down on the three, his bow drawn with an arrow of love and kindness aimed towards each of them.

THE COLOR PURPLE
ALICE WALKER

American author Alice Walker and her 1982 Pulitzer Prize winning novel 'The Color Purple' shows how kindness can be found amid acts of cruelty and the misdeeds of others.

Beginning in America's southern state of Georgia, Walker's novel follows the life of Celie, a poor black girl, who at the age of fourteen is pregnant by her father and suffering under his callousness. Following Celie's life over the ensuing decades, the reader uncovers her continued abuse by others both in the physical and emotional form through the years. Such brutality of spirit is contrasted by the kindness of others given at times during Celie's lifetime, no more so than in those who have learnt compassion through observing Celie's strength of will against adversity, resulting in a new found emotion of kindness brought about in her perpetrators by seeing the error of their ways.

PRIDE

Noun: pride / ˈprʌɪd/
Deep pleasure derived from one's own achievements.
'Her pride was so much she knew everything.'
Synonyms: self-gratification, ego, over self-worth, glory in,
vaunt, boast, brag, crow about, gloat over.

*'Through pride we are ever deceiving ourselves. But deep down below the surface of
the average conscience a still, small voice says to us, something is out of tune.'*

Carl Jung

AN INTRODUCTION TO PRIDE

The complexities of Pride appear in the many forms in which the sin is portrayed.

Observed in the Christian Church as being the foremost attribute in prompting Eve to take the forbidden fruit that played such an intrinsic role in the fall of mankind, foolish pride is also seen as the self-absorbed instinct of those suffering from pride's hold.

A continuing theme in Hindu scripture, many examples of pride abound in the myths of Hinduism, with Indra, King of the Gods, struck with the fearful connotations of arrogance in his proud dismissal of the Divine twins, the Ashwini Kumaras.

Referred to as Hubris both in the Bible and in Greek and Roman Mythology, the sin became an inspiration for artists in the eras of Gothic and Pre-Raphaelite movements.

William Blake's rendition of Hubris took from the parable of Nebuchadnezzar, the Babylonian King so consumed with hubris that his induced insanity caused his reversion of animal instincts within him.

So too did Icarus' pride become subject to artistic portrayal in Draper's The Lament for Icarus in his fall from the skies, his depiction paying its dues to the place of where pride originates from.

Pride in Religion

Christianity

'Live in harmony with one another. Do not be haughty, but associate with the lowly. Never be wise in your own sight.'
Romans 12: 16

Looked upon in the Christian Church, the sin of Pride is viewed as being a preoccupation with the self and the drives that are inherent within the soul of an individual in their eternal wants with no concern for another's wellbeing.

Known throughout history in the theology of Christianity, pride was likened to being the sin of sins due to its connotations in acting as the instigation for Eve to eat the forbidden fruit of the Garden of Eden. Told in the Book of Genesis, an implication of Eve's burgeoning pride in that by in the taking of what was prohibited, it was Eve's pride which spoke of Eden being her and Adam's alone, and so thinking her right to eat from all the abundance surrounding she and her consort.

'The serpent said to the woman, "You surely will not die! For God knows that in the day you eat from it your eyes will be opened, and you will be like God, knowing good and evil."'
Genesis 3: 4-5

The serpents' enticement of being the same as God, aroused Eve's pride further, and so the sin found its first casualty.

The example of Eden's setting for pride to come forth within humanity confirms how pride is observed as a treacherous foe in the Christian belief system. This enemy of the emotions is considered as leading a Christian to assume their position as being that of greater standing than God.

The Catholic Church's view of pride is that the sin acts as a doorway to other sins, namely that of lust and pleasures of the flesh, which is augmented by the attendance of the sin of Gluttony and its joy in seeing humanities deeds of overindulgence, be it in sensual pleasures or that of food, drink and merriment.

The unholy deed of regarding another as being inferior to them is also a transgression of pride. To look down on another who has less in ways of intelligence, wealth or skills, and to gain self-worth from the action is of great distaste to the Church, and displays how a sinner of pride has become so entrenched in the quagmire of hubris. Lacking any kindness for their fellow man and with any measure of humility far out of grasp, an individual strengthens their pride in the telling of their achievements to those of lesser standing, and once more derives pleasure from such activities.

Such is the unpleasantness of the deadly sin, the bitter taste of its features fortifies the words of the 1611 King James Version of the Bible:

'Pride goeth before destruction, and an haughty spirit before a fall.'
Book of Proverbs 16: 18

BUDDHISM

'Why take pride in this body and in possessions, they do not last. They are like the scent of a flower carried off by the wind.'
Gautama Buddha

Buddhism traditions state that Buddha's teachings hold a multitude of instruction on Pride and its failings that hinder the progression of a soul's path towards eventual enlightenment. Translated from the trio of self-satisfaction, egotism and pride, the Sanskrit term for an individual's overestimated self-representation of themselves is Mana.

Mana can be found within many of the precepts presented by the Buddha to be revered by a devotee, be them of the monastic order or that of a Buddhist representative of society. In the Mahayana Tibetan Buddhist tradition, the essence of Mana is identified as being one of the Five Poisons and one of the six Root Unwholesome Mental Factors.

Further to having place in two of the most fundamental of Buddhist instruction, pride's trait of arrogance is represented in the Mahayana tradition in seven different forms.

The Seven Forms of Arrogance in the Mahayana Tradition

Arrogance: The thought that an individual is better than another soul with lesser qualities.

Egocentric arrogance: A mind that thinks only of their own importance in life.

Inflated arrogance: Belief that an individual is better than their teachers.

Unassertive arrogance: Belief in being lesser than another in view of their superior qualities.

Outrageous arrogance: Belief an individual is better than a soul superior in a certain quality.

Untrue arrogance: Talk of attaining a quality that has not been attained.

Distorted arrogance: Belief that a harmful quality such as gambling is a good attained quality.

Pride can also be defined as being a larger-than-life appraisal of the self resulting in a lack of appreciation for those around them. This leads to the ego forming an attachment to the self as seen by an individual under pride's canopy that causes antipathy towards another's soul.

In continuing along a path of pride and arrogance, an individual can encounter feelings of inferiority amongst others. This in Buddhist concerns is believed to lead to the creation of a shield around said individual resulting to isolation from others.

HINDUISM

'Splendour, forgiveness, fortitude, cleanliness, absence of malice, and absence of pride; these are the qualities of those endowed with divine virtues, O Arjuna.'
The Bhagavad Gita

Pride within Hinduism is observed as being one of the six aspects of humanity which prevents a soul from attaining Moksha, salvation.

The six passions of lust, anger, greed, temptation, pride and envy, are transgressions which in Hindu theology are referred to as Arishadvarga.

The Six Passions

Kama: Lust
Krodha: Anger
Lobh: Greed
Moha: Attachment or temptation
Mada: Pride
Matsarya: Envy

It is in the negative characteristic actions of Mada, that pride within an individual soul is expressed as a sin against not only themselves but civilisation also.

With the first two passions of lust and anger, Kama and Krodha, regarded as the instigators of problems experienced in an individual's lifetime, Mada, or pride, takes its place within the suffering of the soul.

Observed as a deepening of selfish behaviour and the development of the false ego, pride is also considered as the main contributor to a Hindu's illusory deception of the self, in that what is achieved through wealth or social standing is believed to be what they are as a sentient being.

This false ego prevents a soul from reaching the expulsion of the ego and so losing sight of the true selflessness of being.

The release of the ego can be achieved in the practice of meditation and in the sacred cultivation of chanting the Lord Krishna's name. In doing so Hindu scriptures tell of the resulting factors of the destruction of sin and a purification of mind, heart and soul.

Mada is regarded as the monster in the sacred Hindu text of the Mahabharata. Known as having great strength due to its physical enormity, Indra the King of the Gods held an inordinate terror towards the beast that was said to able to swallow the Heavens and Earth with one bite of its two mouths.

When Chyavana, a poet who after intense mediation would form his knowledge into hymns, had his youth restored by the twin Divine horsemen the Ashwini Kumaras, in thanks for their gift he told them of a celebration held by Indra where the Gods were to drink Soma, an elixir employed to preserve immortality.

On arriving to the festivities, Indra refused entrance to the twins because of their frequent association with mortals. In hearing such news, Chyavana offered a sacrifice to the twins to symbolise their Godliness, yet learning of Chyavana's offerings a furious Indra reigned thunderbolts down on the poet, only to cease when Chyavana called upon Mada to defend him.

Realising Mada's abilities to swallow the Heavens in one mouthful, Indra relented in the hubris displayed in his forbiddance of the twins and allowed them to partake in his feast.

PRIDE IN MYTHOLOGY

GREEK

Viewed as being a lack of humility and having the characteristics of over confidence and arrogance, Pride is regarded in Greek mythology under the title of hubris.

Both hubris and insolence were referred to as being the attributes of Hybris, the Goddess of Violent acts and Reckless Pride.

Daughter of Erebos the Primordial God of Darkness and his consort, Nyx, the Primordial Goddess of the Night, Hybris was deemed as inciting outrageous behaviour of raucous mortals who had been touched by Dionysus himself, the God of Wine and Merriment.

With Zeus being his grandfather and his twin sister Artemis, the Goddess of Hunting, Apollo, God of Music, Medicine and Plague, was regarded as one of the most pride filled and arrogant Gods.

The traits attributed to Apollo would be told in Homer's The Iliad alongside Niobe who fell victim to her own foolish pride.

Niobe, the daughter of Tantalus, King of the area of Mount Sipylus, married Amphion, the King of Thebes, and bore him fourteen children, seven sons and seven daughters.

Attending a ceremony in honour of Leto, mother of Artemis and Apollo, Niobe's lack of humility and pride in that the celebrations were being held in her husband's kingdom, prompted her to brag about her fourteen children.

Taken as an insult against his mother who had only two children, Apollo took revenge on Niobe's outburst by slaying all seven of her sons.

Joining her brother's slaughter of innocents, Artemis took it upon herself to kill Niobe's seven daughters, leaving Niobe and her King childless. Apollo then proceeded to kill Amphion resulting in Niobe overcome by her loss. Pleading to the gods to be turned into a rock so she may feel no suffering, her wish was granted and she was placed on the side of Mount Sipylus beneath her father's kingdom, where it is said that a stream emerged from Niobe's new form, the water of which is thought to be Niobe's endless tears.

ROMAN

Petulantia was ancient Rome's counterpart to the Greek, Hybris.

Translated from the Latin implying wantonness and petulance, Roman mythology places the Goddess of Pride amongst Deities who showed a similar conceit in their position of immortal life. Born of Nox, the Roman personification of the Goddess of Night, and of Erebus of Darkness, Petulantia's siblings held a series of comparable shortcoming traits to her own likings to arrogance and act of violence against mortal souls. The many Demonises sired of her father Erebus were thought to have come from the same ilk as Petulantia's malicious intents and included Letum, the personification of Doom and the spirit of Death, Eris, spirit of Strife and Discord within humanity, and Querella, the spirit of Mockery and Blame.

Petulantia herself would continue the bloodlines of tormented emotions by bringing Corus, her only son, into the world.

Sharing his mother's fierce attributes of reckless pride, Corus was regarded as the personified spirit of Disdain and Satiety, the revulsion experienced after acts of extreme gluttony.

PRIDE IN ART AND LITERATURE

NEBUCHADNEZZAR
WILLIAM BLAKE

The English poet, painter and printmaker of the eighteenth and nineteenth centuries' Romantic Age, William Blake, depicted Hubris in a number of ink and watercolour renditions under the title of Nebuchadnezzar. The Babylonian King, as told in the Old Testament's Book of Daniel, was said to have had a dream in which he saw a mountain made of gold, silver and other precious metals of the time. On telling the prophet Daniel of his dream it is explained that his vision represented the rise and fall of Kingdoms. Nebuchadnezzar was further told the decent of the wealthy and powerful would begin with the golden effigy of he himself.

Through the King's own pride and fear of the connotations within his dream's prophetic envisions, Nebuchadnezzar fell into insanity and became filled with animalistic behaviours, crawling around on all fours and eating grass in his kingdom's fields like a cow.

Blake interpreted Nebuchadnezzar's psychosis in his famous print, showing the King's eyes wide and filled with madness and directed at the artwork's viewer. Naked and creeping about on knees and elbows, Nebuchadnezzar's unkempt golden beard drags on the floor of his cave like den as he remains lost in the results of pride.

THE LAMENT FOR ICARUS
HERBERT JAMES DRAPER

The 1898 oil painting The Lament for Icarus by Herbert James Draper, portrays the Greek mythological tale of Icarus and his foolish pride in believing he could soar to whatever great heights he believed possible. Architect of King Minos' Labyrinth of Crete, and home to the feared Minotaur, Daedalus, the father of Icarus, built him and his son a set of wings fashioned from feathers and wax.

Instructing Icarus not to fly to close to the sun as its heat would melt the wax, Icarus' pride ignored his father's advice, and so in soaring higher and higher melting wax holding the fathers steadfast melted and left Icarus to plunge to his death into the sea which still bears his name to this day, the Icarian Sea of Mediterranean waters.

Draper's interpretation pictures a dead Icarus laying on a rock amid tranquil seas and encircled by three sorrowful Nymphs. Although in the myth of Icarus' doomed flight it was told he lost his wings, Draper depicts the prideful character as retaining his plume.

Spread out and taking up the majority of the painting, Icarus' wings are displayed in the use of soft tones of ochre and cadmium reminiscent to that of a bird of paradise, the softness and sumptuous tactile representation of which, betrays the harshness of a young man's death, as can be seen in the features of the lamenting Nymphs.

ALL THE KING'S MEN
ROBERT PENN WARREN

Robert Penn Warren's 1946 novel All the King's Men, which would be awarded the Pulitzer Prize for literature one year later, examines pride in it approaching gait towards an individual and its ultimate application to the soul when welcoming the sin into its heart.

When the book's protagonist Willie Stark, a principled lawyer of the American South, changes from an idealistic man into a captivating and bombastic Governor, he receives hubris with all his heart from the result of his embrace of gains from corruption and vice, of which he regards perks of the job for those who have attained that of political high office.

Building an empire of such political power and influence, Stark views himself as untouchable in his pride. The self confidence that accompanies such hubris makes him a hero to the people, yet those within the government see through his arrogance despite the general public's adoration of their champion.

Narrated by Stark's personal assistant Jack Burden, problems arise in Stark's world when he continues in his decent of pride, whilst Burden retains the good morals and humility he held when Willie Stark began his political climb.

THE LAST KING OF SCOTLAND
GILES FODEN

Giles Foden 1998 novel The Last King of Scotland, tells of the dictatorship in Uganda by its tyrannical leader President Idi Amin.

Written as an account by the fictional Scottish doctor Nicholas Garrigan, who gains employment as Amin's personal medical doctor, Garrigan depicts Amin's merciless and cruel dictatorship between 1971 and 1979. It is in Idi Amin's pride of overwhelming self-righteousness that the president sets his eventual downfall in stone.

Captivated by Amin's absolute belief that he is doing right by the people of Uganda, Garrigan begins to fall into the traps of hubris until realising his ethical views on humanity have changed. This proves too late for the young doctor, resulting in a battle of trying to escape Amin's despotic world and triggering the soul's internal fight between right and wrong.

THE SEVENTH HEAVENLY VIRTUE

HUMILITY

Noun: humility / ˈhjʊˈmɪlɪti/
A modest or low view of one's importance.
'Her humility accepted a better way shown.'
Synonyms: humbleness, modesty,
a lack of pride and vanity, diffidence.

'There is nothing noble in being superior to your fellow man; true nobility is being superior to your former self.'

Ernest Hemmingway

An Introduction to Humility

The recognition of another's abilities carries the wisdom that all souls are unique, and so in the understanding of this concept an individual receives stillness of mind that is grounded in modesty.

Even in their lofty positions, overlooking the mortal world, the Gods and Goddesses of mythology portrayed humility as a virtue vital in achieving peace both internally and externally.

Hinduism's King of the Gods, Indra, learnt humility through the acts of reprisal, as did the mortals of ancient Greece when visited by Aidos, the personification of Modesty and Shame.

The endeavours of artists throughout history have portrayed humility as a virtue in it promotion of modesty in the soul.

With the Spanish surrealist painter Salvador Dali depicting the Virgin Mary in her humility as a seated Madonna, in his 1946 painting 'The Madonna of Port Lligat', Dali highlighted the pose that has been rendered in the world of art for centuries.

Ford Madox Brown's painting 'Jesus Washing Peter's Feet', took another view of humility as Jesus kneels down before his disciples and washes the feet of Peter, where observing the act, all present are in awe of their Saviour's modest composure as He displays the humility in the pure sense of love.

The literary world also took it upon them to speak of humility.

Charles Dickens' host of characters in his mid-19th century novel David Copperfield, when portraying the form of false-modesty in that of Uriah Heep and his equally deceitful mother. Yet, this display of the untrue emotions of humilities true essence draws on an individual's understanding of what good values the virtue contains.

Showing humility through poetry, the English author and poet Rudyard Kipling defines a soul's aptitude and attainment of humility in his poem 'If', where he encapsulates one of the many qualities of the Heavenly virtue of humility.

'Or watch the things you gave your life to, broken, and stoop and build 'em up with worn out tools.'
If, Rudyard Kipling

HUMILITY IN RELIGION

CHRISTIANITY

'For everyone who exalts himself will be humbled, and he who humbles himself will be exalted.'
Luke 14: 11

The true essence of Humility in the Christianity is in a believer submitting themselves to God and his teachings with all their heart.

In the practice of humility, the surrender to the Almighty is also recognised as the cultivation of modesty.

The recognition of another's talents and virtues promotes said modesty, which brings with it an understanding of the Christian's own merits and need for humility to play a part in their life.

It is in these actions of recognition of other's attributes that banishes the sin of pride and so that of envy also. This achieved by identifying each soul is unique and has its own talents to offer others, and that the believer's virtues are not the only ones able to bestow such delights and gifts to the world around them.

In the Catholic Church, humility is also seen as guiding a soul towards the action of total surrender to God. The same values of recognition of another's attributes are also found, confirming modesty as the acceptance that all souls are unique, with each one holding its own distinctive talents and abilities.

Humility is closely associated with the Heavenly virtue of temperance. Catholicism regards the values of each in fostering the self-control of boastful actions of a soul's achievements to others, and so influencing the stillness found in humility's territory.

Defined as a virtue of identifying the defects within a soul's own characteristics, it is this identification of the self and its flaws which promotes modesty within the heart, and so nurtures the essence of humility in an individual who recognises another's qualities.

In not adhering to flattery or carrying out deeds which may stimulate the adulation of others in view of receiving praise, humility can be a powerful state in which a practitioner of modesty works within the bounds of his or her qualities and talents, thinking n0t of the fruits such actions may bear. This brings a quietness to the exploration of talents and so advocates a closeness to God.

BUDDHISM

'Reverence, humility, constraint, gratitude and having good Dharma, this is the best good luck.'
Gautama Buddha

Humility is observed in the gaining of higher knowledge through cultivation in the actions with others and in the spiritual practice of meditation and chanting of sacred mantras and scripture.

In all traditions of Buddhism, the fundamental drive and aim is to reach the state of enlightenment, where all suffering leaves the mind and in turn the soul attaining this sacred of positions can help other sentient beings to reach the realms of Nirvana also.

By showing modesty and humility of mind, this leads a Buddhist devotee closer to the attainment of enlightenment and is intensified by the astuteness developed in the experiences of humility and compassion for others and the self.

Advancement in the cultivation of humility can be found in the Tibetan Mahayana branch of Buddhist teaching

A series of Buddhist virtues surmounting to the count of four, the Four Abodes hold instruction in gaining humility to reside in the soul. Known as Brahmavihara, or the abodes of Brahma, this gives to better understanding the virtues and merits of living a life shrouded in modesty to aid a practitioner on their journey to enlightenment.

Brahmavihara - The Four Abodes

Loving kindness.
Compassion.
Empathetic joy.
Equanimity.

It is the first of the Four Abodes that truly identifies humility. By showing benevolence to others, combined with amity, goodwill, friendship and kindness, modesty of heart may be found. This peace within the soul on reaching the sublime state of Brahmavihara's first state is enhanced with expressing an interest in what other souls have to say. These acts of benevolence are entitled Meta and greatly adhered to in Buddhism, means loving kindness.

HINDUISM

'Be humble, be harmless. Have no pretension. Be upright, forbearing; serve your teacher in true obedience. Keeping the mind and body in cleanness, tranquil, steadfast, master of ego. Standing apart from the things of the senses. Free from self; aware of the weakness in mortal nature.'
Bhagavad Gita

Humility in Hinduism is expressed in an assortment of terms. Namrata portrays the essential basis on which the understanding of humility is founded and is translated from the Sanskrit of Hindu sacred text as meaning to be of humble and of modest behaviour.

Other titles in conveying the virtue are Samniti, to show humility towards others, and Amanitvam to hold pridlessness of heart.

Humility's complexities are explained in Hinduism as being not concerned if you receive little or no praise from another and the soul holding no arrogance, false modesty as well as the antagonist of humility, that being of pride.

In respect of the theological concept of showing little concern for praise, humility can be regarded as keeping self-respect towards the self. Coupled with self-control, this facet of humility can be seen in never being impressed by another soul's words of praise directed towards the self.

The self-administered control of the mind, body and soul in matters of acclaim and adoration to actions partaken by a Hindu devotee holds risks of being led astray in such flattery. This leads to the resolution of a believer's soul, in having the strength not to become wrapped up in the pouring of reverence and swept away by the strong winds of adulation.

It is often observed in the foundations of Hinduism that each soul has its own attributes and skills, yet to talk widely of such talents brings with it suffering towards those who may not hold such skills. It is in causing this suffering of others intentionally that breaks the vows of humility and its companion of modesty.

To conceive that another has skills and qualities the self does not show a talent for can bring about modesty within an individual. By cultivating the knowledge that other souls have an equal footing with all souls in the form of talents and abilities, then humility prevails in the understanding of now only submitting to the kindness and power of modesty, but in practicing humility towards others and to the soul of which the humility abides.

In realising these codes of conduct towards fellow sentient beings, it becomes apparent that put simply, all are gifted and all have talents in one way or another.

HUMILITY IN MYTHOLOGY

GREEK

The personification of Humility, Aidos, was regarded by the ancient Greeks in her ability to transmit her other merits of modesty and shame onto a mortal about to commit harm to others. This was applied by bestowing shame upon potential wrongdoers.

The daughter of Prometheus the Titan who aroused wrath in Zeus for his love of humanity that he had fashioned in clay, Aidos' sibling, Deucalion was the first King of northern Greece, and she held a close association with Asia, the Oceanic Nymph and wife of her Titan father.

In the Golden Age of Greek mythology when peace and harmony reigned in the reaches of Athens and Sparta, Grecians looked upon Aidos as granting humility on those who had great wealth and the realisation that their riches came with an element of luck when encountering those of a poorer disposition.

Aidos' attachment to humility was expanded in her companionship with Nemesis, the spirit of Divine Retribution against those who succumbed to the deadly sin of pride.

ROMAN

Being the equivalent of the Greek personified spirit, Aidos, Pudicitia was regarded in Roman mythology as holding the same virtues.

Men and women amid Roman times were expected to uphold Pudicitia's attributes, as her opposing sin of pride was looked down upon with great distaste and repugnance.

So much so that the way a Roman conducted themselves in public was regarded as their conduct of Pudicitia.

Although her counterpart Aidos was mainly concerned with

modesty in the way of treating others with less than themselves, Pudicitia's modesty was regarded as a sensual virtue bordering on the same qualities found in Diana, the Roman Goddess of Chastity.

These further traits of humility's sensual attributes brought unwritten rules concerning the sexual ethics of the Romans, of which was not always adhered to towards the end of the Roman Empire, leading Pudicitia to bear a portion of the blame for Rome's eventual fall from grace in the world.

HUMILITY IN ART AND LITERATURE

THE MADONNA OF PORT LIGATE
SALVADOR DALI

In 1949 the Spanish surrealist painter Salvador Dali created one of his most seminal works.

Inspired by the artistic depictions of the Virgin Mary, he supplemented the virtue of humility in the recognised style of the mother of Christ being seated whilst holding her child.

Portraying the Madonna seated, yet hovering amid levitating marbled alter and cornices, against a barren landscape of blue except for mountains suspended in the air above the distant horizon. Her hands are raised in blessing to the Son of God sitting in her lap while an egg rests above their heads hanging from a thread from the enlarged seashell.

#Using his wife Gala as a model for the Madonna, and the landscape settings from memories of his youth in the north-eastern reaches of Catalonian Spain, Dali's symbolism of the egg in the top centre of the piece denotes new life, whereas the large sea urchin and conch shells to the left signify new beginnings.

The dream like quality of the painting is brought to life in the fact that the Madonna's entire middle torso is absent and is where her new born son now sits.

JESUS WASHING PETER'S FEET
FORD MADOX BROWN

Born in Calais, France in 1821, Ford Madox Brown was an English painter renowned for his representations of historical and Biblical stories.

In his mid-nineteenth century painting 'Jesus Washing Peter's Feet' humility is shown in Christ on his knees cleaning the feet of his disciple, Peter.

With Jesus' head lowered yet crowned by a gold leafed halo, he remains the lowest of the characters Madox Brown depicted, as several other disciples watch on in awe of the act of humility shown to their brother.

Peter himself appears to show humility also in his Saviour's actions, quietly contemplating the message Jesus is conveying to him and those also observing the act of humbleness by someone of held in such great esteem.

Using techniques once attributed to Hogarth, Ford Madox Brown's use of light brings Jesus into focus. This is performed by while the background characters are highlighted in candlelight, Jesus himself is left in stark contrasts against a bright white tablecloth. This use of light goes further as in showing that Christ is glorious, while humble also.

DAVID COPPERFIELD
CHARLES DICKENS

First published as a serial in 1849 and published in its entirety in 1850, Charles Dickens' novel of David Copperfield would feature two souls filled with humility amongst its multitude of characters.

Shortened to the main protagonist's name, the novel's full title goes by 'The Personal History, Adventures, Experience and Observation of David Copperfield the Younger of Blunderstone Rookery (Which He Never Meant to Publish on Any Account)' and is an account of life in the Victorian age, were although humility is deemed a greatest of quality to hold, as in all Dickens' works, all is not what it seems.

When David Copperfield's father is taken ill and dies, his mother remarries. Murdstone, Copperfield's new stepfather, holds a cruel view on how a child should be raised.

When David's mother dies from grief of her losses, Murdstone sends the orphaned Copperfield to London and to work for a living, yet the young David Copperfield escapes to be with his aunt Betsey where he meets with an array of interesting characters.

Mrs Heep shows humility eventually after portraying the virtue in a false subservience in view of getting whatever she desired, and so spending her life in perceived victimhood, although it is her son Uriah who uses the cover of humility to manipulate others into either submission or in the giving up what is desired by the hypocritical Heep.

In Dickens' portrayal of the sycophantic, it is shown how a deceitful portrayal of Humility can act as a veil behind which the sins of lust, greed and pride lurk.

THE LORD OF THE RINGS
J. R. R. TOLKIEN

In J. R. R. Tolkien's three part epic The Lord of the Rings, the Hobbit character of Samwise Gamgee who displays a consistent modesty and humility amongst the strong characters he journeys besides.

On his and his friend's quest to destroy the remaining ring that has caused much suffering to all who it comes into contact with, it is Sam's innocence of being, enshrouded with goodness of heart and the modesty of his chivalrous actions, which defines the Heavenly virtues of humility. It is within his identification of the false modesty of the treacherous creature Gollum that Sam's awareness to the value and qualities of humility prevail, and without effort so too is his own modesty deepens.

This abundance of modesty would be established by the return to his much loved Shire, shown in the guilt experienced towards his newfound heroic stature of which he shied away from, insisting instead his fellow companions deserved more praise than he.

ALSO BY THE AUTHOR

FICTION

SUBWAY OF LIGHT

A novel by Julian Bound

Because Sometimes a Second Chance is All We Need

Following an accident Josh finds himself sat alone at the back of an empty New York subway car on a deserted station with no memory of how he arrived there.

A man approaches and tells Josh he has been taken out of his life to take a journey on the train. Acting as a guide he explains they will make several stops and that each station visited may seem familiar to him.

Arriving at their first stop they witness a young couple meet for the first time. Their ensuing subway stations follow the young couple's life as they experience courtship, marriage, tragedy and happiness. Watching their lives unfold Josh's memory begins to return until it is he himself who must decide the fate of his own final destination.

A story of awakening, 'Subway of Light' is a healing book of love found, lost, and regained through the act of belief and trust, not only within others but also in ourselves.

A heart-warming tale of kindness, understanding and forgiveness.

Life's Heart Eternal

A novel by Julian Bound

One Man's Journey Through The Centuries

'My name is Franc Barbour. I was born on the 20th July 1845 in the town of Saumur, deep in the heart of the Loire Valley, France. The truth of the matter is I simply never died.'

These are the opening words a young nurse reads in an old leather bound journal given to her by a stranger. She soon uncovers the story of one man's journey through the centuries.

From 1845 to present day, and to a backdrop of the world's conflicts and wars, Franc loses then encounters those closest to him again as they are reincarnated time and time again in different bodies.

Be it brothers, friends, soulmates or enemies, those met with once more hold lessons as to how our actions in each lifetime often hold consequences in the next.

In Franc's travels and adventures across the world an encounter with those reincarnated from his past is never far away...

'For who has never wondered what it would be like to live forever?'

THE GEISHA AND THE MONK

A novel by Julian Bound

Two souls born thousands of miles apart
each shall follow a similar path

KYOTO, JAPAN 1876

A girl is born into a lineage of famous geishas. She is taken to a renowned Tokyo geisha house where her training to serve and entertain others begins.

GYANTSE, TIBET 1876

A boy is born into a small rural community. Recognised as the reincarnation of a revered Lama he is taken to live in Tibet's legendary Tashi Lhunpo Monastery.

SAN FRANCISCO, USA 1900

At the dawning of a new century fate brings them together, a lifetime away from all they have ever known.

Set against a backdrop of the streets of Tokyo and within the high altitudes of Tibet, *The Geisha and The Monk* follows the parallel life stories of a Tokyo geisha and a Tibetan Buddhist monk, who although coming from very different backgrounds share a matching destiny, a destiny revealed on the shores of San Francisco's harbour front.

'Eventually, two souls destined to meet shall do so, their connection instantly recognised within the eyes of the other.'

THE SOUL WITHIN

A novel by Julian Bound

In releasing our thoughts towards a lifetime imagined,
only then may we have the life our soul awaits.

Falling ill in his home town of Puri on India's eastern shoreline a young boy is visited by a mysterious woman. Taking him on a journey around a tranquil lake, together they observe those living along its banks.

Acting as a guide the woman explains the life lessons they encounter through gentle teachings. As the boy begins to realise the significance of their walk his emerging awareness to matters of the soul leads him to discover the true reason behind their meeting.

A heart-warming tale of awareness, The Soul Within provides readers with an insight into awakening, guided by subtle teachings grounded in love, kindness and compassion.

OF FUTURES PAST

A novel by Julian Bound

Past lives and reincarnation, one soul's journey

Following her death, a young New York art restorer finds herself on a deserted beach. An older man approaches and introduces himself as George.

Explaining she is now between lives, George guides her to a cliff top library. Inside she finds a book containing all the past lives she has ever lived. She begins to read of her past lifetimes lived throughout the centuries.

Be it an artist's model of 16th century Renaissance Italy, a geisha of ancient Japan, or a Tibetan Buddhist monk living in the foothills of the Himalayas, each lifetime holds answers towards the progression of her soul, as seen in those met with through the years, be them friend or foe, or ultimately her soul mate she encounters in her many lifetimes.

Between uncovering the events of her previous lives, George explains the reasons for the situations that unfolded within her past. His explanations provide awareness to characteristics unique to her soul, and of the trials she at times has been faced with.

Of Futures Past is a story of discovery, giving an insight into how our actions in one lifetime can effect moments in those to follow.

A Gardener's Tale

A novel by Julian Bound

'It's funny the people you meet in a lifetime.
Looking back it wasn't so much how many crossed my path,
more so it was what they had to say.'

With these opening lines a sheltered man recounts his life spent working as a gardener in his hometown's park. Recalling those encountered he tells how they shared their problems with him, resulting in him offering them his own unique perspective on life and so touching the hearts of all he meets.

Unbeknown to them all, his wise insights for their woes arrive from the numerous jigsaw puzzles he and his mother complete together each the evening. Yet as tragedy strikes, it is he who must search for the missing piece within his own life puzzle.

Because Everybody Searches For Their Missing Piece

By Way Of The Sea

A novel by Julian Bound

One monk's journey of discovery

Struggling with his beliefs, Tenzin, a Tibetan Buddhist monk, begins a journey to see the sea he has always imagined. Travelling on foot through Tibet, Nepal and India to reach his goal, those he encounters along the way start to restore a faith lost to him.

Since a young novice Tenzin has longed to stand before seas never witnessed in a landlocked Tibet. Travelling through his homelands he walks beside holy lakes and over high attitude mountain passes until stepping into Nepal, where within the gardens of Buddha's birthplace his fading beliefs begin to be rekindled.

Crossing into India he journeys south once more until meeting with a path he is destined to take.

Encountering many on his travels each hold a valuable lesson for Tenzin as together they explore the concepts of attachment, impermanence, kindness and compassion and karma and reincarnation. With each insight gained he continues onwards, his pursuit to see the sea accompanied by a want to understand the faith in which he has been raised.

FOUR HEARTS

A novel by Julian Bound

'You walk into a room filled with all the people you've ever met, who do you seek out first?'

Diagnosed with an incurable illness, one man begins a journey across the world to meet with those from his past.

Travelling to India and Nepal's ancient cities and to Thailand's tropical islands, those he encounters hold a message for him. Exploring the concepts of love, friendship and heartache it is he who must ultimately face a destiny shaped by life choices made.

Four Locations, Four Souls, One Journey. - *'Four Hearts'* a tale of wanderlust and self-discovery.

ALL ROADS

A novel by Julian Bound

A journey of awakening in the foothills of the Himalayas

When Josh's intended two month holiday in Thailand heads in an unexpected direction the doors of a new world are opened to him.

Pulled away from his comfort zone and led across South East Asia by a turn of surprising encounters and events, he finds himself in locations never thought of before.

From Thailand and Cambodia's golden temples to the banks of China's Li River, and from the high altitudes of Tibet's ancient monasteries to Nepal's sacred lakes, Josh gains insights into Asia's Buddhist concepts and principals while walking a path he is destined to take.

OF EDEN'S TOUCH

by Julian Bound

Tales of Horror in Paradise

Beware when in paradise, its delights are often not what they seem...

From the remote Himalayan monasteries of Tibet and Bhutan, to Nepal and the backstreets of Kathmandu, and from the isolated bamboo forests of Japan to encounters with the macabre in India and China.

Chilling stories of entities and spirits roaming across Asia and South East Asia - some lost, some choosing to stay on the borderlands between life and death... others intent on sharing their malevolence with any passing traveller happened upon.

**Ten chilling tales of horror,
with each carrying a unique twist and bite.**

Countries Featured

Thailand, Japan, India, Cambodia, Bhutan, Tibet, Myanmar, Nepal, Indonesia, China

NON-FICTION

IN THE FIELD

A Memoir by Julian Bound

Tales of capturing world events, conflicts and culture on camera whilst living on the road as a documentary photographer.

From the boy soldiers of a Burmese liberation army to photographing the moment Nepal's 2015 earthquake struck, *In The Field* tells of Java's active volcanoes, Cairo's Arab Spring, Bangkok's coup d'état, and a venture into covert photography for a government in exile.

Alongside tales of conflict and natural disasters another journey is recounted, one of documenting Buddhism throughout Asia and South East Asia, including Bhutan's fortress monasteries, Tibet's remote temples, chanting Tantric monks of the Himalayas, and meeting His Holiness the 14th Dalai Lama at his 80th birthday celebrations.

Stories Featured Include

The Karen National Liberation Army
Nepal's Maoist Civil War
Rebellion on the streets of Bangkok
Tibetan refugees
A journey through Tibet
Mumbai's Dharavi slums
Cambodia's Killing Fields
The Nepal earthquakes of 2015
His Holiness the 14th Dalai Lama

TEN MINUTE TRAVELS

by Julian Bound

35 short stories of travel and adventure set across 20 countries from National Geographic photography contributor Julian Bound.

From Tibet's high altitudes of a Mount Everest base camp to encounters with sharks on Fiji's coastline, and from earthquakes in Nepal to a meeting with His Holiness the 14th Dalai Lama in the foothills of the Himalayas, each story tells of life on the road with a backpack, camera and a huge dose of wanderlust.

The Mindfulness
of Wandering

by Julian Bound

21 Mindful Walks through 7 Buddhist Countries for Reducing Stress and Anxiety and Finding Peace of Mind in your Everyday Life

Calm the mind and start a journey towards finding peace with twenty-one short mindful walks through the beautiful temples, gardens and shrines of Asia and South East Asia.

Finding peace in today's modern world can be difficult. Although calm appears at times in our daily lives it is often fleeting, allowing elements of stress, anxiety, sadness and at times exhaustion to take dominance again. By practicing mindfulness in our day to day activities of work or play a once elusive peace can become a constant.

The Mindfulness of Wandering guides a reader towards being in the present moment through cultivating awareness to our surroundings. Each mindful walk is designed to encourage observing the world around us with curiosity and accepting things for how they really are in a non-judgmental way.

From Tibet's high altitude temples to Cambodia and Thailand's golden shrines, and from Japan's bamboo forests and tranquil gardens to India's sacred Himalayan pathways, every walk takes a reader on a journey through nature and sights seen within the comfort of mindfulness' embrace.

Take a journey in mindfulness today and transport yourself into peace.

ABOUT THE AUTHOR

Born in England, Julian is a documentary photographer, film maker and author. With photographic work featured on the BBC news, his photographs have been published in National Geographic, New Scientist and the international press. His work focuses on the social documentary of world culture, religion and traditions, with time spent studying meditation with the Buddhist monks of Tibet and Northern Thailand and spiritual teachers of India's Himalaya region.

His photography work includes documenting the child soldiers of Myanmar's Karen National Liberation Army, the Arab Spring of 2011, Cairo, Egypt, and Thailand's political uprisings of 2009 and 2014 in Bangkok.

With portraiture of His Holiness the 14th Dalai Lama, Julian has extensively photographed the Tibetan refugees of Nepal and India. His other projects include the road working gypsies of Rajasthan, India, the Dharavi slums of Mumbai, the riverside squatter slums of Yogyakarta and the sulphur miners at work in the active volcanoes of Eastern Java, Indonesia.

Present for the Nepal earthquakes of 2015 he documented the disaster whilst working as an emergency deployment photographer for various NGO and international embassies in conjunction with the United Nations and the World Wildlife Foundation.

With published photography books Julian is the author of nine novels.

Made in the USA
Monee, IL
09 October 2023

44282671R10097